growing
food in small
gardens

Reprinted in 2011
First published in 2010 by New Holland Publishers (UK) Ltd
London • Cape Town • Sydney • Auckland

Garfield House
86–88 Edgware Road
London W2 2EA
United Kingdom
www.newhollandpublishers.com

80 McKenzie Street
Cape Town 8001
South Africa

Unit 1
66 Gibbes Street
Chatswood
NSW 2067
Australia

218 Lake Road
Northcote
Auckland
New Zealand

ISBN 978 1 84773 696 3

Senior Editor: Corinne Masciocchi
Designer: Geoff Borin
Illustrator: Kate Simunek
Production: Laurence Poos
Editorial Direction: Rosemary Wilkinson

10 9 8 7 6 5 4 3 2

Reproduction by Pica Digital PTE Ltd, Singapore
Printed and bound by by Times Offset (M) Sdn Bhd, Malaysia

Barbara Segall

growing food in small gardens

NEW HOLLAND

contents

introduction

FOOD MILES — THE DISTANCE THAT FOODSTUFFS TRAVEL ON THEIR WAY FROM THEIR PLACE OF ORIGIN TO A SUPERMARKET NEAR YOU — ARE PART OF EVERYDAY PARLANCE AND ALTHOUGH THE JOURNEY IS NOW AMAZINGLY QUICK COMPARED WITH WHAT IT USED TO BE, IT STILL TAKES DAYS OFF THE FRESHNESS OF THE FOOD. IT IS A SIMPLE FACT THAT BY GROWING FRUIT AND VEGETABLES YOURSELF, YOU CAN ENJOY THEM AFTER THE SHORTEST POSSIBLE TRIP BETWEEN HARVEST BASKET AND PLATE. BECAUSE YOU ARE THE HARVESTER, YOU CAN PICK THE FRUIT AND VEGETABLES AT THEIR PEAK, RATHER THAN A FEW DAYS PAST THEIR BEST.

As you are the gardener, you can decide the amount of chemical intervention used to control the inevitable pests and diseases that will vie with you to devour your produce. Whether you are 100 per cent organic or choose to use a little pesticide, at least you will know how the plants have been grown.

I first started growing vegetables when I lived in a flat in London. I had a small allotment so soon mastered the art of growing quantity in a limited space. Although I now have a large country garden, I still grow my vegetables in small rectangular raised beds, within flower borders and amongst herbs and edible flowers. I have particular vegetable favourites and grow tomatoes, pumpkins and courgettes (which demand larger spaces), beans and year-round salad leaves as my main crops each year.

In this book I have selected some of the varieties that have given the best results for my small spaces and provided the basic information you need for your first foray into urban kitchen gardening. The book covers the techniques for preparing the soil, producing the plants and outlines the small spaces that you are likely to encounter. It also provides practical suggestions for making those sites both productive and ornamental, and offers some design suggestions for particular situations. Growing your own vegetables is one of gardening's great pleasures. Kitchen gardens have evolved from purely practical production areas attached to large houses into ornamental yet productive gardens for everyone. Ornament comes in foliage colour, shape and texture, in flowers and fruit, and in the combination of crops and garden designs. Picking fresh crops through the year provides high nutrition, taste-packed rewards unmatched by supermarket produce.

LEFT Here a balcony wall provides shelter for low-growing or mound-forming herbs such as creeping thyme, sage, chives, parsley and borage. They are growing in a specially constructed, deep planter, running along the outer edge of the balcony. The herbs are combined with ornamental plants such as the silver-leaved Senecio.

Success on a small scale

Small-space vegetable growers are skilled in the art of filling every bit of the garden with productive plants. In addition, they have perfected the art of using vegetables and herbs rather than flowers to beautify their small vegetable areas. In a large garden the vegetable patch – seen by some as more functional than attractive – is often kept out of sight, separated from the flower garden. In the small garden where space is at a premium, this segregation is an out-of-place luxury.

Even in the smallest city garden, there is sufficient space and opportunity for the determined fruit and vegetable grower to plant a wide range of produce. Window boxes, containers of all shapes and sizes, hanging baskets and grow-bags are among the challenging sites

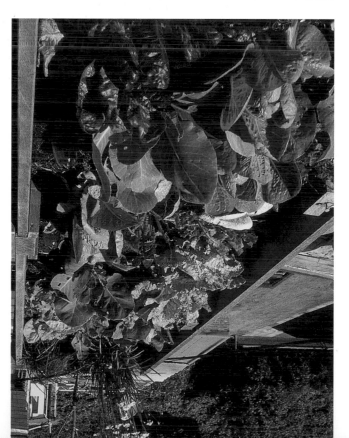

ABOVE Lettuces keep close company with cauliflowers during the early stages of growing. By the time the cauliflowers mature and fill out, the lettuces will have been harvested.

for the urban kitchen gardener. The small-space vegetable grower has to adopt one or two strategies to ensure a regular supply of vegetables that suit the site and their own appetite. Fresh produce, straight from the garden to the plate is the prize, and in a small garden it is won with a combination of work and ingenuity.

Planning and making the choices that suit your taste buds and garden spaces are the keys to success in the small city vegetable garden. Plants may have to work hard for their place, providing good flavour, ornament and nutrition. Effectively they become double-duty plants, providing a double function of ornament and use. For example, instead of growing an apple tree which will take up a fair amount of space, plant a row of low-growing apples trained into cordons to form a step-over hedge (see page 77). This will provide attractive flowers in spring, abundant delicious and attractive-looking fruit in autumn and will make a useful boundary for part of the garden.

choosing crops

Small-space gardening has several advantages over large-scale gardening, and with clever planning you can keep a succession of fresh, home-grown produce ready for harvest through the year. But you do have to make choices. You have to decide what you will grow, how and more importantly where you will grow it. Then you have to manage the sowing and growing so you have a regular supply of seasonal food throughout the year.

The first rule is to plant what you enjoy most. Fresh leaves for salad mixes, edible flowers and various coloured lettuces may be your summertime choice, while for winter you may decide that you cannot live without a daily pick of spicy oriental salad leaves. Of course, if there is a particular vegetable or fruit that you would eat on a regular basis, glut or no glut, then plant that in profusion.

Bulk produce and large, thuggish plants such as cabbages which take up a great deal of space will not be options for the small-space vegetable gardener. In small spaces growing large quantities of anything will not be possible, and in any case, that would defeat the object of the fresh fast food you are harvesting.

Vegetable growing is seeing a resurgence in popularity and seed companies around the world are promoting a wide range of vegetables. Many of them offer small vegetable plants for sale, relieving the small-space grower of the early part of the crop production. The choice of vegetables and fruit and especially of old, flavour-filled heritage varieties on offer is particularly exciting.

Harvest gluts can become very boring; at first it is great fun having vegetables in abundance to offer neighbours and friends, but then eventually they too will be overwhelmed. When there is a glut of one particular vegetable, not only do you get tired of eating too much of it, even when it is at its freshest, but freezing or otherwise preserving it becomes a chore too. So small quantities, harvested over time, are best.

growing for health

We all know that eating vegetables and fruit is good for you, but one added bonus of growing your own is the exercise you will have digging and delving in and around your vegetable garden, helping to burn off calories and keep you in good shape.

The list of essential vitamins and minerals on the opposite page will help you decide which vegetables to grow.

Vitamin A (antioxidant, good for the immune system and for night vision) is converted in the body from yellow-orange and red vegetables, and leafy greens including carrots, lettuce, parsley, peppers, spinach, squash and tomatoes.

Vitamin B (unlocks energy) is found in aubergines, broccoli, cauliflowers, courgettes, lettuce, parsley, peppers, squash and tomatoes.

Vitamin C (antioxidant, boosts immune system, protection against cancer and cardiovascular disease) is found in broccoli, Brussels sprouts, cabbages, cauliflowers, green beans, lettuce, parsley, peppers, potatoes, spinach and tomatoes.

Vitamin E (antioxidant) is found in green beans, peas and leafy greens.

Calcium (strengthening bones) is found in beans, broccoli, lettuce, parsley, peppers and tomatoes.

Iron (conductor of oxygen to cells) is found in lettuce, oriental greens, parsley, peas, spinach, and tomatoes.

Magnesium (nervous system) is found in beans, broccoli, cucumber, lettuce, peppers, potatoes, tomatoes, and squash.

Manganese (frees up proteins and fats) is found in beetroot, carrots, lettuce, peas and watercress.

Potassium (maintains fluids in cells) is found in aubergines, beans, broccoli, lettuce, carrots, cauliflowers, courgettes, cucumbers, oriental greens, parsley, peppers, radishes, spinach, squash and tomatoes.

Selenium (antioxidant, protects cells, boosts immune system) is found in beans, peas, sweetcorn and many other vegetables.

Zinc (DNA synthesis, cell division, growth) is found in beans, lettuce, parsley, peppers, potatoes, spinach and squash.

ABOVE Every space in this garden has been used to good effect for productive and ornamental purposes. There is still room for a table and chairs to enable its owner to enjoy the garden's harvest.

chapter one:

improving the soil

Preparation
Soil types
Soil in containers
Potting compost
Composting and mulching
Wormeries
Watering

sowing and growing

Germination
Sowing in containers
Plant plugs
Successional planting

pests and diseases

Common pests
Diseases

small kitchen gardens

Sun, shade and shelter
Air circulation
Making a plan

rooftops and balconies

First considerations
Screening and shelter

patios and courtyards

Practical pointers
Container gardens

1

getting started

THE DEMANDS OF A SMALL KITCHEN GARDEN DICTATE THAT IT MUST BE AS ATTRACTIVE AS POSSIBLE AND YET ALSO FULL AND PRODUCTIVE. THERE ARE A NUMBER OF STRATEGIES FOR ACHIEVING THIS. EVERY SPACE, NO MATTER HOW SMALL, IS A PLANTING OPPORTUNITY.

small kitchen gardens

IF YOU ARE FORTUNATE ENOUGH TO HAVE A GARDEN, HOWEVER SMALL IT MAY SEEM, YOU WILL BE ABLE TO GROW A GOOD PROPORTION OF YOUR OWN VEGETABLES, HERBS AND FRUIT.

Most urban gardens are tucked away behind terraced or row houses and are of a roughly uniform shape and size. Long and narrow, with boundaries usually marked by fences or walls, they are in effect small outdoor living spaces, with varied demands put on the space by the different family members. If you are lucky enough to allocate as much as possible of the garden for vegetables you can plan for a traditional, albeit small-scale, row vegetable garden.

Even if you are only able to carve out a small square, rectangle or circle for the vegetable garden, it will still provide you with a range of fresh vegetables and fruits if you choose the varieties carefully and prepare the soil well. If you have to share your vegetable passions with other garden demands, it is likely that the area for vegetables will be to one side, with a wall or boundary of some sort, at the back of the site.

With a proper garden, you will be able to plant directly into the soil, but you will have to prepare the soil well, especially if the garden has not been cultivated previously (see pages 20–1). However, many small gardens suffer from the effects of countless feet trampling them and compacting the soil. This will mean that it will be very difficult to work the soil into a good state. The solution is to make raised beds (see pages 34–5) filled with loam-based compost and well-rotted manure, and leave to weather over the winter.

You will need a number of tools, some big and bulky such as hoses and lawn mowers, and others, such as forks and spades, that can be placed in specially designed store cupboards, some of which double as garden benches. If you have the space for a small greenhouse or propagating unit, this will allow you to make sowings ahead of the warm weather.

LEFT A small rectangular bed on a patio will provide a quantity of produce. Herbs, such as chives and parsley, offer light shade for a row of lettuces, while dwarf beans, sugar snap peas and broad beans planted in short rows are ready for harvest in early and midsummer.

sun, shade and shelter

When choosing where to site the vegetable plot, consider the garden as a whole.

• Track the sun and note the persistently shady areas of the site. Position the plot so all plants benefit from maximum sunshine and taller plants or climbing plants such as beans don't overshadow low-growing plants. Some vegetables and herbs thrive in shady conditions but the majority need the sun to make them grow and to fill them with flavour and nutrients. Most vegetables need at least six hours per day in the sun. Lettuces and many salad leaves, as well as a few herbs, are the exception, preferring light shade.

• Also assess the site for shelter. Vegetables need open, sunny positions, but they also need shelter from drying and damaging winds.

• Pick a site where the vegetables are not competing with trees or hedges for the water and nutrients in the soil.

GARDENER'S TIP

Use walls, arches or pergolas to support climbing plants, such as thornless blackberries or runner beans, to make most efficient use of space.

ABOVE *All available space in this garden is well used. Fruit grows against the fence and archway, while borders and beds are filled with produce.*

air circulation

Good air circulation is important for fertilization of some crops such as sweetcorn, and open airy sites will also be relatively pest- and disease-free. However, strong wind is the vegetable grower's nightmare as it is the source of great stress for plants. Its action causes windrock, which in turn loosens the root's grip on the soil, from where the plant derives its major source of vital water and nutrients. It also increases the rate at which plants lose water. This is a natural process, but if it happens too quickly, the plant will weaken and may collapse before it can replenish moisture levels.

To provide shelter, especially on rooftop gardens, patios and other exposed situations, you need to use lightweight material such as bamboo panels, which will look attractive when in place. Remember, though, that screening materials, however lightweight and non-competitive they may be, are likely to reduce light and moisture that would normally be available to the plants. Site screens carefully so that they don't shade the plants from their necessary daily quota of sunlight. Hedges, while offering shelter, also compete with vegetable plants, so either you will have to provide plants with extra nutrition or use lightweight, man-made or natural materials.

GARDENER'S TIP

If you are working on a new piece of ground which hasn't been cultivated before, you may need to remove turf and dig the ground. This is best done in autumn when the ground is still workable and it allows it to weather over winter. Any compost or manure you work into it will also be well incorporated by the action of weather and the activity of soil organisms (see pages 20–1).

TOP If you have cut beds from a previously turfed area, the ground needs to be well dug and compost or manure added to improve the soil's texture and fertility.

ABOVE In this compact kitchen garden, paths are vital to provide access to the vegetables in the boarded, raised beds. They also add a pleasing visual neatness to the garden as a whole.

BELOW A rectangular shape divided by paths becomes a four-square garden. By siting the beds away from the hedges, you can access them easily.

making a plan

1 Before planting up the plot, draw a sketch of your garden to scale and decide where the various beds, hedges, paths, seating and so on will be best placed.

2 Once the sketch is complete, mark its shape out on the ground, using pegs and string lines or with a line of sand, so that its actual position and size is apparent. Consider the layout from all angles and make any necessary adjustments.

3 Put in place the hard landscaping (paths, stepping stones, and so on) and the raised beds (wooden boards or brick-built beds), if relevant to the design.

4 Avoid compacting the soil by working on wooden boards laid over it to spread your weight.

rooftops and balconies

IF THE ONLY SPACE FOR YOUR VEGETABLE GARDEN IS ON A ROOFTOP OR BALCONY,

A FEW PRACTICAL CHALLENGES WILL NEED TO BE DEALT WITH BEFORE YOU CAN START.

First of all, there will be no natural soil available and access to the roof or balcony will limit what you can transport, either with help or single-handedly. Whatever you need to get started – plants, soil, containers, decking and propagators – has to fit into the lift or you need to be able to carry it. You may need to enlist help to get your roof or balcony garden going. Everything has to be transported up stairs or in lifts to the top of the building, in the case of roof gardens, or to a number of levels if the site is on a balcony. And on the return journey, any garden waste or debris has to come down in the same way and be disposed of safely.

Nonetheless, there is plenty of scope for growing vegetables in a wide variety of containers, and for adapting the space to house some permanent designed structures such as raised beds or decking. However, on rooftops these may be subject to planning permission and to structural constraints.

ABOVE *Hot peppers set taste buds tingling and enliven the view from a balcony. They may need staking or shelter if the area is windy.*

RIGHT *A glass screen offers permanent shelter on a windy balcony, yet does not reduce light levels. In addition, it provides a private spot to enjoy in apple blossom time, as well as at other times through the year.*

first considerations

Weight Before you begin a rooftop or balcony garden, make sure the structure can take the weight of the containers you are planning. On balconies and rooftops the outer edges are structurally the strongest areas, so it is wise to arrange containers around the edges. If you are able to construct raised beds (see pages 34–5) to run around the boundaries of your roof or balcony space, this will be the safest option and will also provide the plants with the shelter of the adjacent walls.

Surface material You will also need to take into consideration the material that covers the surface of the roof or balcony. Many flat roofs are sealed with tar which can become extremely hot in summer and large heavy pots will leave marks in it. A solution is to fit a raised decking over the whole or parts of the roof. This will keep the plants cooler in their pots and will mean that the roof surface is not damaged.

Sun and shade Just as for a ground level garden, you need to track the sun and establish where the shade is and where the hot spots are.

Drainage On balconies you will need to consider the neighbours downstairs when you are watering the containers. A muddy waterfall spilling from your balcony to another will not endear you to your neighbours. As far as it is possible, only water directly into the containers and place water-holding saucers under pots.

screening and shelter

City rooftops and balconies on different levels provide limited spaces with great views. Like country landowners, city gardeners on high levels can 'borrow' the landscape' around them. These potential growing

ABOVE Even on the smallest rooftop there is the opportunity to grow a range of vegetables in attractive containers. Individual kohlrabi plants will be replaced by more of the same, or a different crop, such as lettuces.

sites are usually facing similar balconies and rooftops that return the gaze and see your balcony as 'the view', so you may feel that you need the privacy offered by screening.

Wind protection Rooftops and balconies are notoriously windy so the screening will also help to make the site more sheltered for your plants. Exposure to wind can be reduced by using lightweight screening material and growing the climbing plants on it to get maximum value out of every bit of space. Many rooftop spaces are enclosed by walls on several sides and these can be used to support lightweight netting systems to hold beans and peas which will thrive in such sheltered positions, as well as lower-growing plants such as tomatoes, peppers and potatoes.

patios and courtyards

IN TERMS OF SPACES AND SHAPES, PATIOS AND COURTYARDS PRESENT THE SAME SORT OF CHALLENGES AS BALCONIES AND ROOF GARDENS. THE DIFFERENCE IS THAT AT GROUND LEVEL, THERE ISN'T THE WORRY ABOUT WEIGHT AND THE NEED TO TRANSPORT EVERYTHING UPWARDS.

ABOVE A raised platform on a patio doubles as a planting area and is framed by a row of herbs and salad leaves with pots of herbs and beans running the length of tiered staging.

practical pointers

Access The consideration of access remains a key factor, especially if the only access to the courtyard or patio is through the house and not by means of a side entrance. If you plan to include a large structure, such as a garden bench or an arch, either choose a flat-packed style or measure doorways or narrow passageways carefully first.

Aspect Patios and courtyards are often shaded by neighbouring or opposing buildings, only receiving sun in the middle of the day. However, surrounding buildings will also offer shelter and this can protect the site from frost and wind. You can also increase the light and warmth of the patio and courtyard space by painting walls white to reflect the sun.

Raised beds As these areas are often paved or have a concrete floor, growing in raised beds or containers is the solution (see pages 34–5 and 44–51). Once you have overcome the logistical difficulties of balconies, rooftops, patios and courtyards, you will find many opportunities for using containers inventively, and decorative as well as productive plantings will be limitless.

Container gardens

On a rooftop, balcony or patio you won't need to draw a paper layout of the site, but the same principles apply.

- Sit down on the patio or roof garden and see which areas are the sunniest, where the prevailing wind is and work out where to place climbing plants and containers for salads so that they benefit from the best available positions.

- You may well wish to make a sketch highlighting the different containers that you plan to use and to draw up a planting checklist.

- It is unlikely that you will have a greenhouse so you may need an indoor site for seed sowing. If you do have the space on the roof garden or patio for a tall, shelved seed-sowing unit, you will be able to raise many of your own plants.

ABOVE A productive climbing gourd grows over the fencing in this sheltered, plant-enclosed patio, where vegetables and nasturtiums mingle with ornamental plants, such as shaped box in containers.

improving the soil

THE SOIL, AND ITS HEALTH, ARE OF PARAMOUNT IMPORTANCE TO THE QUALITY OF THE FOOD
AND THE QUANTITY OF THE YIELD YOU ARE LIKELY TO PRODUCE IN YOUR KITCHEN GARDEN.

preparation

Autumn is the best time to prepare the site. Soil that has
not previously been used for vegetable growing needs
double-digging to aerate and open it up. If possible, you
should also dig in well-rotted manure and home-made
bulky organic compost (see page 22). These elements
will enrich the soil and encourage the activity of micro-
organisms and beneficial insects and invertebrates. There
are some vegetable crops such as potatoes that will be
good to grow in previously uncultivated soil. You can also
improve the soil's overall fertility by applying chemical
fertilizers, by growing and digging in green manures and
by adding bulky organic matter to the soil when you dig
it over in autumn.

soil types

There are four types of soil — sandy, loam, clay and chalk
— and each has different attributes and will support a
range of vegetables. However, to grow a wider variety
in a particular soil you may need to improve or change
your existing soil. A slightly acid soil with average fertility
and a high organic content will satisfy the widest choice
of fruits and vegetables.

Light, free-draining soils are very useful for producing
early crops but because of their structure they lose
nutrients and moisture quickly. You can improve this
by adding a standard fertilizer and working in organic
matter when you dig the soil in autumn.

ABOVE A well-balanced soil that has been dug over in autumn with
compost added will provide the perfect environment for a wide range
of home-grown vegetables.

Heavy clay soils are either too wet or too dry. In wet periods they become sticky and waterlogged, while in hot dry periods they crack. In spring they are cold and take longer than a sandy soil to warm up. In time you can improve them by adding abundant organic material, horticultural grit and sharp sand.

For high yields, soil needs to have an open, aerated structure and it should hold moisture and nutrients for the roots. First and foremost, keep off the soil yourself. You can do this by growing vegetables in raised beds or beds that you can work from the sides, rather than walk on the plot itself. If you have to walk on the soil, use wooden boards so that you don't compact the soil.

ABOVE *To keep the soil in good health, avoid walking directly on it. Use wooden boards as temporary walkways between rows, so that you can work from them. They will also suppress weeds.*

soil in containers

It is best to use a proprietary potting compost where the nutrient level and structure is measurable, as opposed to digging up soil from the garden. In the garden plants will be able to reach and use the available nutrients and moisture, but once garden soil is used in a container it is difficult to quantify the amount of nutrient and there may be deficiencies or diseases. To make sure your container vegetables are receiving their nutrient quota you will have to provide it in the form of liquid fertilizers or through slow-release fertilizers added at the time of potting up.

potting compost

There are two types of compost, loam-based and soilless, each with its good and bad points.

Loam-based compost will support a good range of food plants. However, it is heavier in weight than soilless compost, which can be problematic on balconies and roofs and may make it very difficult to move containers around easily.

Using a weightier compost can be an advantage, provided the roof can cope with the additional weight, as loam-based compost does provide stability in the pot for the plants. It releases nutrients over time, is free-draining and has a good structure. All this makes for good establishment of healthy productive plants but has to be set against the weight factor.

Soilless compost Peat is the main ingredient of soilless compost. Other materials include grit, shredded bark or coir and vermiculite, all of which improve the drainage. It is lighter than loam-based compost, but is less stable. It is not as moisture-retentive, so when a soilless compost dries out it is difficult to re-wet it satisfactorily.

Composting and mulching

If you have space, install a compost bin or make a small area of the garden into a compost site.

- Place the compost bin, usually made out of plastic, on well-drained soil in a sunny site, close to the vegetable plot.

- Add any kitchen vegetable and fruit peelings (high in nitrogen and carbon), tea leaves, coffee grounds, crushed eggshells, prunings from other plants, and vacuum-cleaner dust.

- If you have garden waste such as weeds (as long as the seeds are not ripe), evergreen clippings or leaves, you can add these as well.

- You should not include any diseased plant material, cooked food (it will attract rodents) or the faeces of domestic pets.

- Add different types of material in layers and from time to time add activators or accelerators that will add nitrogen to the heap and heat up the compost so that it decomposes more quickly. There are natural activators, such as uric acid, farmyard manure, seaweed, comfrey and grass clippings, as well as many commercial activators available in liquid or powder form. You may not need to add an activator, but in colder weather or winter it will help to speed up the process.

- Keep the lid on your compost heap or cover it with a piece of old carpet to retain heat and moisture and to protect it from rain. If the compost become very dry, add sufficient water to moisten it (but don't saturate it). For example, a heap or bin 30–60 cm (1–2 ft) in depth may need several large watering cans.

- The compost is ready to use when it has changed into a friable, crumbly mixture that resembles the proprietary compost blends available from garden centres. You will be able to dig this into your containers and into the garden or use it as a mulch around plants.

Mulching (covering the surface of the soil with straw, compost, bark or leaf mould) reduces water loss from the soil surface, keeps it warmer and lessens annual weed germination rates.

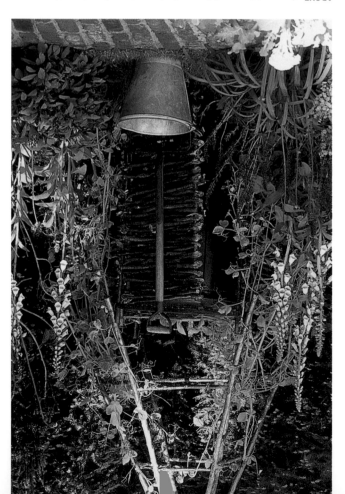

ABOVE *Compost is one of the garden's most precious harvests. Following the small-space principles of ornament and beauty, camouflage a plastic compost bin with a wooden hurdle and a wigwam of sweet peas.*

wormeries

It will be difficult to keep a successful compost bin going in the limited space of a balcony or a roof garden, but if you have the space a wormery will provide liquid fertilizer as well as friable compost. Wormeries take up a small amount of space and can be fixed to a wall. They are relatively clean and easy to assemble and use. Green-fingered children are likely to be very good caretakers of the whole system.

A wormery is a unit of stacking or tiered containers used to house a collection of worms which will turn kitchen waste into compost. The worms will eat their own weight of waste each day transforming it into a concentrated liquid fertilizer and a solid, soil-improving compost. The liquid can be drained off daily once the wormery is established and used, diluted, according to the instructions that accompany the wormery. The highly nutritious solid material can be used to improve the soil. Keep the wormery in a frost-free site during the winter.

watering

For convenience, the site needs good access to watering facilities. If necessary, think about laying in an irrigation system which can be computerized or automated. This can be a large investment but it will pay off in the long term. In a container vegetable garden on a roof or patio,

a watering system can be invaluable, especially if timed to come on and off several times a day to give plants regular watering. Plants take up water from the soil in the ground or in containers through their roots and in hot periods or when seedlings are establishing it is vital to add to the reserves of water in the soil.

Whether you grow vegetables in containers or in the ground, always make sure you water the ground or the potting medium, rather than the whole plant. Keep a reservoir of water in a plant saucer, under the plants in containers and whatever you do, avoid spraying over the leaves. In sunlight this will result in leaf scorch.

ABOVE The soil conditioner here is home-made compost produced in a tumbling composter: I held above the ground on a metal frame, the bin is turned frequently so the material inside is well mixed.

sowing and growing

germination

Seeds need warmth to germinate. Most seed packets will give an indication of when you should sow seeds direct into the ground, but remember that this is a general instruction and you should always make an adjustment for your particular micro-climate. If you can sow seed indoors to get a head start, don't start too early or you will be inundated with seedlings which will soon become leggy if it is still too cold to plant them outside. Most vegetable seeds can be sown directly into the ground, but many half-hardy plants, such as tomatoes, aubergines, cucumbers and basil, will need to be started off in a propagator or on a warm sunny windowsill. In general they will need a temperature of 10–21°C (50–70°F) in order to germinate. You will need to keep a sunny windowsill in action during the year if you are sowing in succession and need replacements for vegetables as they are harvested.

Carrots, beetroot, parsnips and radishes can be sown directly into the ground or into containers and you can thin out as they mature.

ABOVE Harden off seedlings sown indoors by gradually acclimatizing them to outdoor conditions in a coldframe over a period of days. Make mini-greenhouses from cut-away plastic bottles, which will provide frost protection for young plants.

sowing in containers

1 Use containers such as seed trays or cellular sowing trays and fill them almost to the top with soilless compost.

2 Flatten the surface with a piece of board, then moisten the compost using a watering can with a fine rose or a mist sprayer filled with water.

PLANT PLUGS

Many seed companies offer individual seedlings and small plants each grown in a tiny 'plug' of compost. The range offered is wide, and these young plants are ideal for gardeners who don't have a greenhouse or propagator. It could be argued that on their journey through the mail to you they will have endured root disturbance, but by the time they reach you they will have gone through all the difficult stages in a young plant's life and are less likely to suffer from damping off (the fungal disease which can wipe out a whole collection of seedlings soon after germination). They will establish quickly once you plant them into their growing sites.

Plant plugs are usually accompanied by growing instructions, but the most important step is to remove them from their packaging and, if they need water, apply it carefully and sparsely and plant them up as soon as possible. Orders are usually despatched to coincide with the correct time for you to plant out.

3 Sow fine seed thinly onto the surface of the compost and barely cover with a layer of compost, sow larger seed deeper into the compost. If you are using a cellular tray, sow one or two seeds into each cell. Cover large seeds such as tomatoes with compost.

4 Place the newly sown seed trays in a propagator or cover them with a polythene bag and place on a sunny windowsill. Check the compost regularly but don't overwater.

5 Once the seeds have germinated, remove the propagator lid or polythene bag. When the seedlings are growing strongly, bring them into more direct light and water to keep the compost just moist.

6 When the seedlings have grown large enough to handle you can prick them out into larger pots. You may need to harden them off – put them outside during the day and bring them indoors at night until they have adjusted to the outside temperature.

If you have sown seed into cellular sowing trays or other small containers, wait until two true seed leaves are showing and the seedlings are just large enough for you to handle before you plant them into their growing positions. Handle gently as any damage will result in a shock to the plant's system and a setback in its growth.

successional planting

Successional planting is a useful technique that helps to extend the growing season. Staggered sowing or planting of vegetables such as lettuce which, if sown in one go will all come to readiness at one time, is the key to success. As one crop matures and is harvested, another is well on its way to replace it. Gardeners describe this as 'sowing a little and often'. This method requires a series of 'understudy' plants, waiting in the wings, ready to take centre stage when the current plant has been harvested.

pests and diseases

ALL PLANTS IN ALL GARDENS – WHETHER CULTIVATED AT GROUND LEVEL OR HIGHER UP,

IN BEDS OR IN CONTAINERS – ARE LIKELY TO SUFFER FROM PESTS AND DISEASES AT

SOME STAGE IN THEIR DEVELOPMENT.

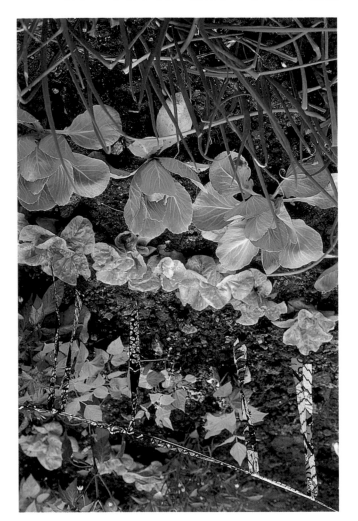

ABOVE Coloured ties and old CDs which glint in the sunlight are among the unusual and inventive measures adopted by gardeners to keep birds off vegetable crops.

The cleaner you can keep your tools, the site and your pots, the lower the chances are for devastating infections or pest problems. Whether you use alternative or mainstream chemical sprays to control pests and diseases, make sure you read the manufacturer's instructions and follow them carefully. There are many alternative treatments available and you can also select vegetable varieties which are resistant to particular pests and diseases, minimizing the chance of infection.

There are also some useful techniques like companion planting of flowers that will attract predatory and pollinating insects which will have a beneficial effect on the pest situation. Many gardeners use French marigolds inter-planted with tomatoes and brassicas, the poached egg plant (*Limnanthes douglasii*) and fennel, to attract hoverflies which control garden pests.

There are numerous protective materials such as netting for covering soft fruit bushes to guard the fruit against birds. Some gardeners use stylish scarecrows or make their own bird-scarers. There are black cat faces with glowing eyes which can be inserted into vegetable rows or into containers to imitate cats and thus ward off birds. Humming lines (plastic tapes which, when pulled taut between canes, make a sound to deter birds) are also useful and in some high-tech gardens unwanted CDs are strung onto lengths of wire or string and recycled as glinting bird-scarers.

common pests

Aphids

Greenfly and blackfly are different types of aphid. They damage plants by clustering on stems, leaves and buds and sucking the sap of the plants. They can overwhelm plants or simply cause distortion to stems and shoots and may also bring virus infections with them.

- They can be removed and crushed by hand (wear gloves if you are squeamish).
- Otherwise, dislodge them with strong blast of water, or spray with a solution of insecticidal soap.
- Natural predators include ladybirds, which are drawn in by their presence, and hoverflies which are attracted by fennel flowers and poached egg plants.

Cabbage root fly

This fly's maggots attack the roots of all brassicas including kohlrabi, kales and broccoli, boring into the roots. It is at the seedling or transplant stage that the crop is most vulnerable.

- Protect the plants with barriers such as special brassica collars on the ground at the plant's base or a covering of horticultural fleece until the plants are well established.

Carrot fly

The maggots of this fly attack carrot, parsnip and celery roots. The fly is attracted by the smell of the foliage when it is crushed, so if you thin the seedlings or weed around them, this is sure to attract the pest.

- Avoid the need to thin by spacing seeds further apart at sowing time.
- Use carrot fly-resistant varieties, such as 'Fly Away'.
- Erect a barrier of plastic or fleece that is at least 75 cm (30 in) high.

ABOVE Aphids.

ABOVE Cabbage white caterpillar.

Caterpillars

Caterpillars eat the foliage of many plants and can be picked off by hand.

- Check the foliage, especially on the undersides, for the caterpillars.
- Also check the undersides of the leaves for eggs and squash these.

Flea beetles

Flea beetles damage the foliage of many vegetable plants, including brassicas and peas, making small holes and weakening, even overwhelming seedlings. Healthy, strong plants are not as susceptible.

- Sow in good conditions so seedlings can establish.
- Cover the crop with a fleece barrier.

Onion fly

Onions, leeks and shallots are vulnerable to the maggots of this fly which will bore into the bulbs and stems.

- Crop rotation (see page 28) minimizes the chances of onion fly spreading.
- In addition, try to grow your onion crop from sets rather than from seed, as they are less likely to be affected than seed-raised onions (see page 64).

CROP ROTATION

In a small space you might be tempted to grow the same crop in the same place year on year. However, this is likely to lead to a build-up of the pests and diseases that affect the particular crop in that part of the garden. Crop rotation can be a useful method. The basic principle is that you divide the available space into four sections and move the vegetables according to the group they come under into another section each year, in a four-year cycle. (If you are not growing brassicas, ignore them as a group and simply divide the area into three sections and rotate three groups over a three-year period.)

1 Vegetables in the first group are the legumes and include peas, beans, and all plants with podded fruits. Sweetcorn is also included.

2 Brassicas, including broccoli, cabbages, cauliflowers and kale, make up the second group.

3 The third group includes root vegetables such as beetroot, carrots, parsnips, potatoes and turnips. Include tomatoes and peppers too.

4 The fourth group is the onion tribe which includes shallots, leeks, garlic and chives. You can include courgettes in this section as well.

Red spider mite

The symptoms are small yellow and white markings and webbing on leaves. They are prevalent in hot, dry greenhouses and may be more of a problem for container-grown vegetables than in the ground.

• In greenhouses, use predatory mites, *Phytoseiulus persimilis*.

• In the open and in containers make sure plants are well-watered in dry periods, if necessary misting the foliage of container-grown plants in the evening or when they are in the shade.

Slugs and snails

These invertebrates damage the foliage and young shoots of most vegetables, including lettuces and brassicas.

• They are large enough to be picked off and removed by hand.

• There are other barrier methods such as crushed egg shells, gravel and other uneven, sharp materials that can be placed around the plants to deter the slugs and snails.

• Slug pubs – a dish, yoghurt carton or specially bought container – can be filled with some leftover beer, the smell of which attracts the slugs, which fall in and drown.

Vine weevils

Vegetables cultivated in the ground are not likely to be attacked by vine weevils, but if you use soilless compost for vegetables grown in containers, check it for fat white grubs.

• Remove and destroy any you find (do not throw them on the compost heap).

• You are less likely to encounter this pest in loam-based compost, although fruit grown in containers is susceptible.

• Use nematodes to control them outdoors in spring and autumn.

ABOVE Slug.

ABOVE Red spider mite.

diseases

Apple and pear canker
The symptoms of canker are distorted sections of wood and black patches that appear on the skin of fruits.
• Control by pruning out affected sections of wood.
• Remove and destroy the damaged fruits.
• Choose the modern canker-resistant varieties and improve soil drainage.

Blight
This affects potatoes and outdoor tomatoes. It is most likely to occur in damp, humid weather and can damage the plants very quickly.
• Use resistant varieties.
• Improve the air circulation around the crop by increasing planting distances.
• Always remove any affected plants, and dispose of them or burn them.

Clubroot
This organism affects brassica roots, resulting in weak, unhealthy, stunted plants.
• Avoid it by rotating crops.
• Lime the soil (always follow manufacturer's instructions).
• For a small planting of brassicas add ericaceous compost to the planting trench. This will increase the acidity, which brassicas prefer and as it is fresh, is less likely to harbour the organism.
• Always dispose of affected plants.

Damping off
Poor hygiene, including the use of rain water and old compost, results in this fungal attack which may overwhelm young seedlings and plants. Signs of it include the stems rotting and turning black and the plant dying off.
• Only use water straight from the tap and always use fresh compost for seed sowing and transplanting.
• Sowing the seeds too close together can also encourage damping off.

Downy mildew
This fungal disease shows as a fluffy, shadowy outline on leaves of brassicas, lettuce and onions.
• Make sure there is good air circulation around plants.
• Remove any affected parts and keep the area weed-free.

Grey mould
Poor hygiene and cool, damp growing conditions will increase the likelihood of grey mould occurring on above-ground parts of the plant.
• Remove affected plants (or just the affected parts).
• Don't wet foliage when watering.

Powdery mildew
Courgettes and brassicas are particularly susceptible to powdery mildew, which is prevalent in dry weather. A white fungal growth appears on the upper leaf surfaces.
• Water regularly in dry periods.
• Improve air circulation and good garden hygiene.

Rusts
Leeks are prone to rust, which appears as bright orange spores on the leaves.
• Remove badly infected parts of the plant, and clear away.
• Keep water off the leaves.
• Improve hygiene.

Silver leaf
This disease affects stone fruits such as cherries, plums and greengages. It occurs if the wood is damaged or pruned at the wrong time.
• Summer pruning reduces the chance of the tree succumbing to it.

Viruses
Viruses affect vegetables such as cucumbers, courgettes and marrows and result in stunted unhealthy plants.
• Choose resistant varieties.
• Destroy affected plants as disease will spread through to others in the row.

chapter two:

traditional rows

raised beds

decorative planting

paths and walkways

2

garden layouts

THE WAY YOU PLAN YOUR VEGETABLE GARDEN WILL DEPEND ON THE SPACE AVAILABLE;

THERE ARE MANY WAYS TO GET THE MOST OUT OF SMALL SPACES. WHETHER YOU

GROW VEGETABLES IN TRADITIONAL ROWS OR IN THE FLOWER BORDERS,

THE RESULTS WILL BE PRODUCTIVE AND ORNAMENTAL.

traditional rows

LINEAR OR STRAIGHT ROWS OF PRODUCE ARE THE TRADITIONAL CHOICE IN MOST VEGETABLE GARDENS, AND MAY BE THE BEST SOLUTION FOR MAXIMUM USE OF THE AVAILABLE GROUND.

advantages

It is simplest to sow seed into straight rows and, as a general rule, rows are easier to maintain. Weeding is easier if plants are all growing in one axis as the weeds can be easily identified and hoed off. It is also more convenient to water along rows without wetting foliage and if you need to warm up the soil or protect plants, standard cloches are more likely to fit the average row.

Traditional row-growing needs more space than other systems, and produces more of a particular crop. In the row system you need to have space between rows and between plants within the rows and it is these requirements that take up the space. The minimum space between rows is 15 cm (6 in), the maximum is 45 cm (18 in), depending on whether the vegetables are small, large or greedy feeders which need more space. However, there are many other ways to divide the space, or rather, to manage and arrange the vegetables.

short rows and blocks

You don't have to fill a long row with just one type of vegetable – you can split rows and in a long thin town garden, short rows, where you sow vegetables in blocks of several short rows, may work best. This also looks

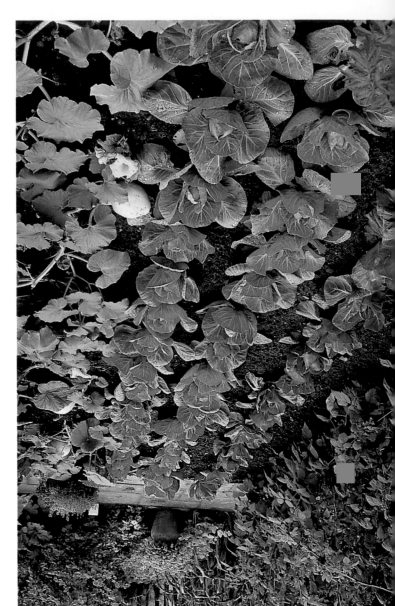

LEFT In a traditional vegetable row each crop is grown in a long line, with regular spacing between rows. It is easy to keep rows weed-free by hoeing down the lines.

wide rows

Wide row planting is a system favoured by many American gardeners, including Californian garden writer Rosalind Creasy, author of *Edible Landscaping*. In this system rows about 1 m (3 ft) wide and 5 m (15 ft) long are either dug into the ground or are contained in a raised bed (see pages 34–5). The long wide bed can be worked from the paths and edible flowering plants are used as companions to make the garden look attractive, to aid pollination and also to use in salads.

close spacing

Mini or baby vegetables widely available in supermarkets are 'designer' crops, small enough to provide the flavour of their full-size relatives and fun to grow in containers and small urban gardens. They can be grown by planting ordinary varieties very close together and picking them before they fully mature. There are also many varieties that have dwarfing characteristics or have been bred to produce mini-versions of their larger mainstream relations (see page 68).

intercropping

Intercropping is another way of getting the most out of a small space. This technique is used in any intensive cropping system and involves combining crops which have differing growing times. Carrots and parsnips will take longer to reach maturity than radishes which can be successfully inter-cropped with them, that is planted

in the spaces between rows of carrots and parsnips. The radishes will be ready to harvest ahead of the carrots, and by the time the carrots are getting larger, and needing more of the nutrients and moisture available, the radishes will be out of the ground. The intercropping regime can continue with, for example, a sowing of lettuce into the space left by the radishes.

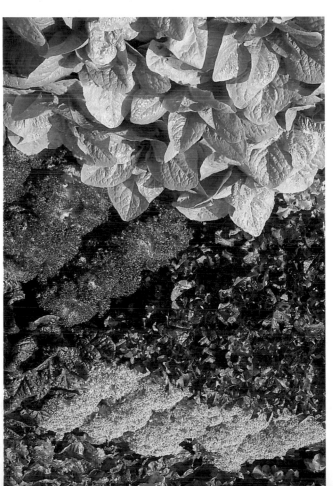

ABOVE *Close planting looks very attractive and by harvesting alternate plants you can prolong the display.*

attractive, as you have sections with different shapes, colours and textures of vegetables. And it means that you can make repeat or successional sowings at a future point in time.

raised beds

DEFINING THE VEGETABLE GARDEN'S LIMITS WITH RAISED BEDS PROVIDES SMALL SPACES THAT ARE USEFUL FOR MAXIMUM CROPPING AND IDEAL FOR COURTYARD OR ROOFTOP GARDENS.

practicalities

Raised beds can be brick-built or have their sides enclosed with wooden boards or railway sleepers. With this method, the soil is effectively raised above ground level. Good organic material can be worked in. In these small spaces, plants may still be arranged in rows, but planting distances are reduced, keeping weeds in check and allowing you to produce more plants. You could also adopt any of the other bed layouts suggested in this chapter.

soil

The soil within the raised bed needs to be dug over and prepared well (see pages 20–1), then additional material from the compost heap (if you have one) is added. The width of the raised bed is critical: any wider than 90 cm (36 in) and it will not be possible to work the centre without stepping onto the soil. And that is the whole point of this gardening system – it doesn't need the space between vegetable rows for walking on or working from. This means the soil will not be damaged or compacted by you and if enriched regularly with compost, will go on producing healthy, tasty vegetables over a long period.

FOUR-SQUARE GARDENING

This is a technique devised by American vegetable gardener Mel Bartholomew for growing many crops in small spaces. The basic size of the area is a square 1.2 x 1.2 m (4 x 4 ft). The square is further divided into sixteen 30 cm (1 ft) squares. Make yourself a grid system with string or wires laid across the large square. Each small square is used for a different crop, or you can use several squares for a particular crop. This gives an attractive patchwork effect. In production terms it enables you to grow many more plants and the basic shape will fit into a small garden. The square is enclosed by four wooden sides, so becomes a raised bed which you fill with a mix of garden compost, potting compost and vermiculite. Each time a square is harvested, replenish the compost to refresh the soil and plant another crop. The planting is carefully managed so the tallest crops are grown at the back or on the north side of the bed and don't shade the lower crops. This means all the plants get the same amount of sunlight. Giant vegetables aren't possible in this system but you will get a crop of tasty smaller vegetables, and weed and pest control is easy from the sides.

Back row
- Sugar snap peas 'Oregon Sugarpod' or
- Runner beans 'Prize Winner'. Use all four small squares to ensure a reasonable harvest.

Second row
- Kohlrabi 'Purple Delicacy': four plants.
- Onion sets (either 16 for smaller onions or nine for larger onions).
- Lamb's lettuce can be sown later on direct into the square for a winter salad crop.

- Beetroot 'Monogram' (either 16 for small beets or nine for larger individual beetroot).
- Leeks 'King Richard'.

Third row
- Dwarf runner bean 'Hestia'.
- Carrot 'Parmex' or 'Early Nantes': broadcast the seed or sow in three rows and thin out.
- Turnip 'Milan Purple Top' (sow in two rows or broadcast over the square).
- Dwarf French beans: four plants, 'Purple Teepee' or 'Royally'.

Front row
- Parsley: either plant in nine small pots for a full look, broadcast or plant in three rows.
- Lettuce 'Little Gem' or 'Red Salad Bowl': sow into three rows or transplant 16 seedlings or young plants.
- Rocket: broadcast seed over the square or sow into three rows.
- Cut-and-come-again lettuce: sow into three rows.

LEFT *Raised beds are particularly useful on patios or courtyards where a reasonable depth of a workable soil is otherwise difficult to achieve. Here an attractive log edging provides a decorative touch.*

decorative planting

IN A SMALL GARDEN, WHERE THE VEGETABLE PLOT IS ON SHOW, IT IS IMPORTANT TO MAKE THE BEDS LOOK AS ATTRACTIVE AS POSSIBLE. THERE ARE SEVERAL DIFFERENT WAYS YOU CAN ACHIEVE THIS. THE FOLLOWING IDEAS CAN BE USED IN RAISED BEDS OR AT GROUND LEVEL.

dual-purpose planting

In row-gardening (the slightly disparaging name given to traditional vegetable gardens), the plants thrive in long lines, are harvested and the ground then lies fallow, waiting for the next crop. In small space gardening, the rows are turned into decoration, with planting blocks in short rows or in squares grown in ever-diminishing squares within each other. This is essentially growing in rows, but rows with a difference.

Edgings In the same way, you can grow a crop, such as parsley, lettuce, chives or even leeks, as the double-duty decorative and productive edging for a bed of other vegetables. Keep the row attractive when you harvest by replacing with new plants or by harvesting in a sequence, say of every other plant. In this way the decorative edge won't disappear all at once.

Beans and peas can be used to provide temporary cover or screening on a patio or a roof garden. Bean flowers are attractive and peas and beans in pod offer a wide range of colour combinations, as well as tastes after harvesting.

Hedges and dividers Think even bigger and turn hedges into productive plantings. Fruit trees, such as apples and pears, can be trained into architectural shapes, so that they fulfil a structural function as well as a productive one. For example, step-over apples (see page 77), at just 45 cm (18 in) high, provide a boundary marker for the

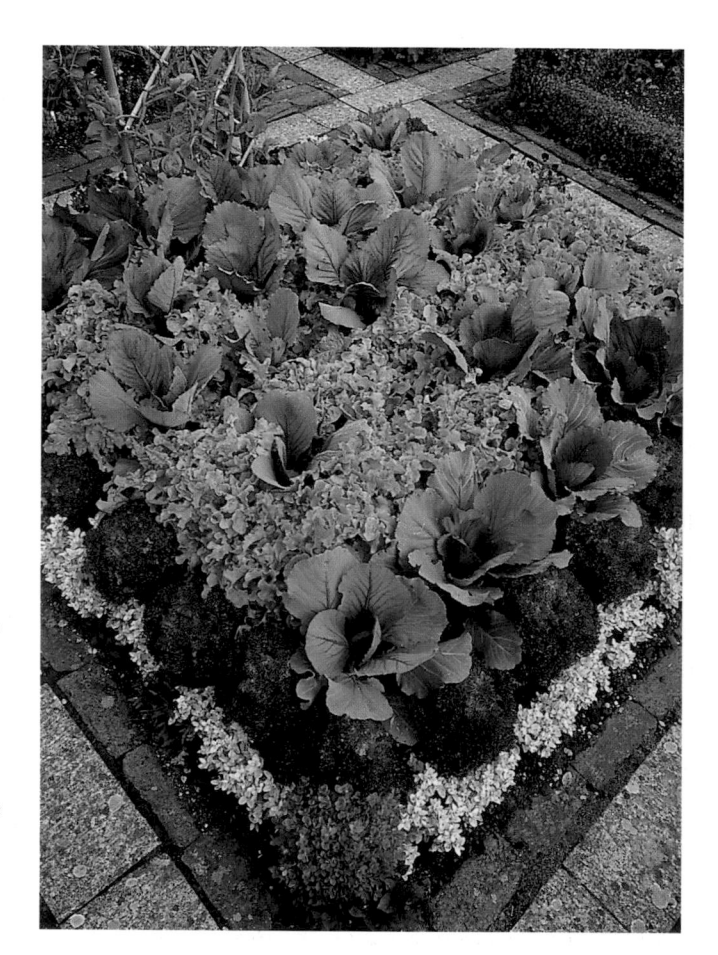

ABOVE *Here the colourful foliage of cabbages and lettuces combine with that of golden and green box plants to make a dazzling ornamental display. The productive qualities of the plants are secondary to the aesthetics, although by the time the cabbages need more space the lettuces will have been harvested.*

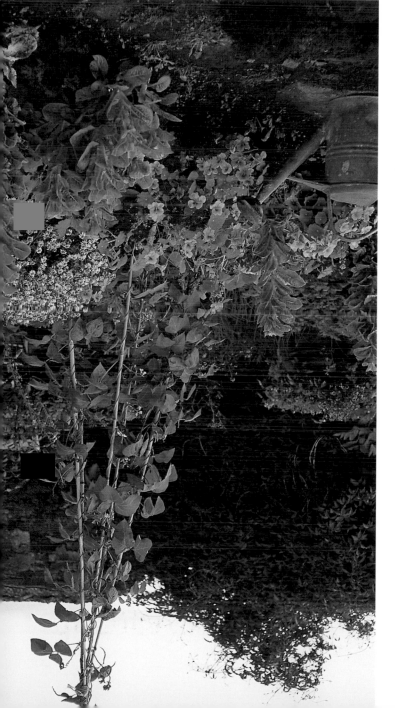

ABOVE Many vegetables look attractive in a border. Here runner beans add height and lettuces have been left to set seed. Although the lettuces are too bitter at this stage to harvest, they still offer colour and shape.

potagers

Colourful flowers, attractive foliage and bright fruits are among the decorative attributes of many vegetables. Ornamental vegetable gardening now has a great following. Described as potagers, these gardens combine production with aesthetics. Usually arranged within small formal, box-edged beds, the vegetables are chosen for their visual attractions and the overall effect is of a tapestry of texture and colour. They are also combined with flowers and shrubs.

Among my choices here are some of the cabbage family which I would normally consider too large to be worthwhile in the small space kitchen garden. These include red kale 'Redbor' which, with its deeply indented and striking red-purple foliage, makes a dramatic border plant.

colour scheming

You can choose vegetables primarily for their taste, but the colour and texture of their leaves and the shapes in which they grow, are factors in the mix. Lettuce, providing crunch and crispy texture, whether planted in rows or in containers, comes in a rainbow wave of wonderful colours, from bright apple-green through to translucent pinks and purple. Chard, whose stems and leaves are delicious simply blanched and brushed with butter, is available in white-, yellow-, and red-stemmed

Soft fruit can also be grown for a dual purpose. Choose standard gooseberries for height and shape, as well as their fruits. Use thornless blackberries on fences or arches, or grow blueberries and figs in containers on a patio or balcony.

fruit and vegetable garden but also provide both produce and ornament and veined forms, all of which are striking. Beetroot foliage, delicious when young in salads, comes in a green and purple veined combination as well as in a matt purple.

climbing plants

Climbing and vining plants, such as beans, peas, grapes and some squash and gourds, need support. In the small space garden this offers you another opportunity to use the vegetables for that extra double-duty of ornament and function. For some plants such as pumpkin and squash this may be the only way that you can include these space-eaters. Gourds are naturally vining and, if offered upward support, will scramble up and cling to an archway or other strong structure.

Metal arches are suitably strong supports for heavier plants such as grapevines, thornless blackberries and pumpkin or squash vines.

Formal structural garden features such as wooden or iron obelisks can be used to support vegetable climbers but when covered in beans or vines, their own intrinsic structural impact will be hidden from view.

Supports for beans are usually in the shape of a framework of canes arranged either in long, double rows, with canes crossing and secured at the top with canes running the length of the row, or round, wigwam arrangements of canes. However, there are variations and the canes can be arranged as uprights, with string wound between them to support the bean plants as they grow. Try rustic sticks or poles as an alternative.

Peas will also need support but shorter canes or a series of woody branches hung with pea netting will be sufficient.

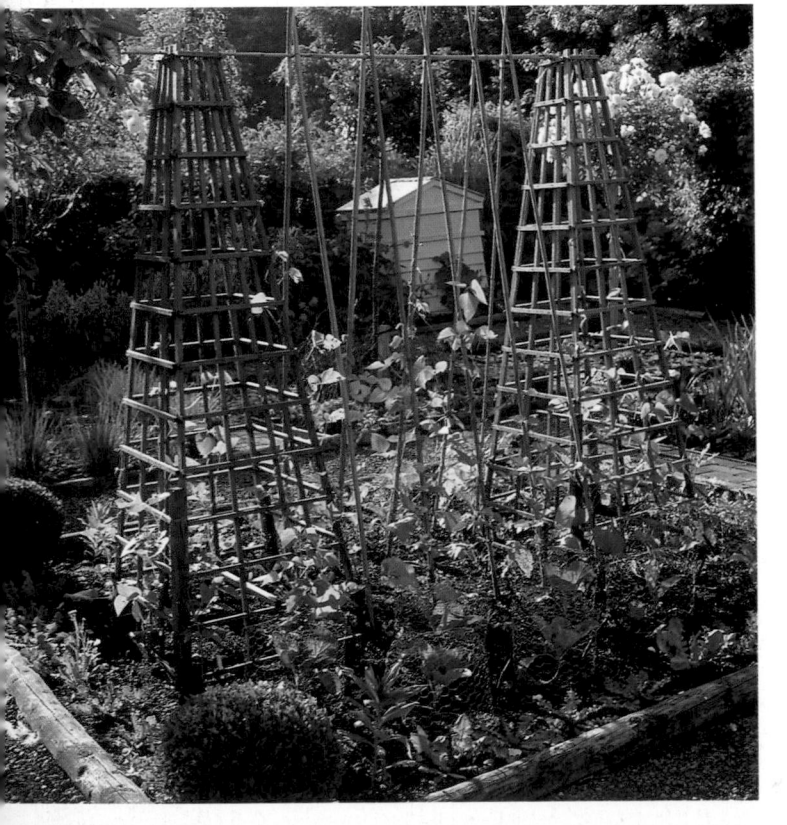

LEFT *Beans and other climbing vegetables need a framework. In the small garden this can be achieved using many different attractive support systems.*

RIGHT *If there is not enough space to grow pumpkin and squash on the ground, provide plants with a strong metal or wooden support, such as an iron archway or an old climbing frame, and they will happily scramble upwards.*

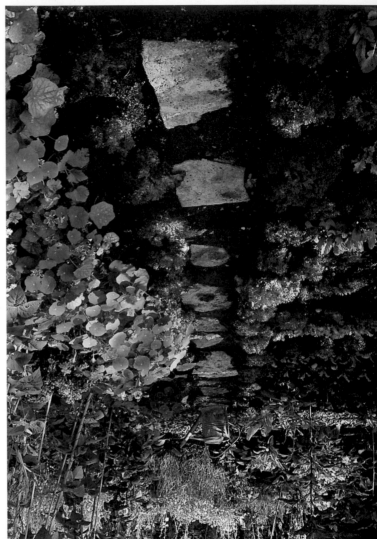

paths and walkways

paths

Garden paths can be made from a wide variety of
materials including gravel, sand, bark chippings or pavers.
Old bricks in mellow, weathered colours can be laid in
a traditional herringbone pattern, while slate chips look
attractive and very modern. The simplest paths consist of
straw or bark chippings, laid directly onto the soil. You
can make the layers as thick as the available straw or bark
chippings will allow. It will be 'walked' around and flung
about the garden by birds, but is easily reconsolidated.
Stepping stones can be placed into the planting area,
so that you can get straight into the garden to work.
If possible try to keep off the soil so that you don't
compact it, making it impervious to water. This will
mean that water doesn't drain away well, so roots will
not have even access to water and young plants may
be swamped by too much water at their necks.

bed edgings

Natural materials are also useful to make decorative
edges for the vegetable garden, separating the beds from
the paths. They take up very little space and yet offer
definition to the garden. Choose materials to

LEFT Stepping stones placed at intervals across a vegetable garden
provide access and still leave much of the soil free for planting.

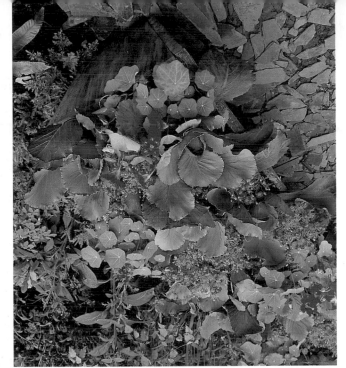

complement the paths. For example, if the path is made from bark chippings, twiggy pieces of curved willow stems become a lightweight barrier, to keep plants off paths and people off the plants. Hazel twigs woven together offer a similar effect.

RIGHT Slate chippings laid onto a well-constructed path offer extra and often complementary colour for ornament.

ABOVE Tile boards that enclose a raised bed help to keep the leaves at the edge of the planting off the ground, as well as hold the path material off the soil.

chapter three:

movable feasts

Aesthetics
Weight considerations
What to choose
Planting up a container
Growing potatoes in a barrel

window boxes, grow-bags and hanging baskets

Window boxes
Grow-bags
Planting a hanging basket
Support for grow-bags
Watering tips

3

growing in
containers

THE CONTAINER ENTHUSIAST WILL SEE EVERY BOX, POT, TIN, BASKET OR PLASTIC
BUCKET AS A POTENTIAL VEGETABLE-HOLDING POSSIBILITY. THE VARIETY OF
CONTAINERS IS VAST, RANGING FROM TRADITIONAL TERRACOTTA AND
RECYCLED HOUSEHOLD ITEMS TO MODERN GALVANIZED IRON.

moveable feasts

BY USING CONTAINERS, YOU CAN MOVE PLANTS THAT ARE AT THEIR BEST TO THE FOREFRONT
OF THE PLANTINGS, AND WHEN YOU HAVE HARVESTED THEM, THEY CAN BE REPLACED WITH
NEW STARS.

aesthetics

Containers are an essential element in the small-space
vegetable grower's repertoire. On patios and balconies
they are often the only available growing sites, and on
the ground they offer focal points and provide height,
for what is an essentially low-growing palette of plants.
Arranging the containers can be as much part of the
artistry of the vegetable garden as are the decisions as
to which vegetables and varieties to grow for the
maximum ornamental and productive value.

Growing plants in containers is labour-intensive
and not the cheapest way of producing vegetables since
you have to supply all the plant's needs, and you have
to be on hand to water and feed on a regular basis.
Plants growing in the ground can get their water and
nutrients through their roots from what is available in the
soil, but for container-grown plants, what you give them
is all they get. However, in small spaces where you are
close to the plants, it is easy to spot pests and diseases at
an earlier stage and, if possible, to remedy the situation.
One advantage is that you can be completely assured
of organic produce.

weight considerations

When planted up, some containers will be too large
to be moved around and should be used as permanent
growing sites. The weight of containers once filled with
the plant and compost, and especially when watered, is a

ABOVE Terracotta 'pouch' pots are among the most popular containers
for vegetables and herbs. Provided it is relatively deep, it is possible
to grow several different plants, such as parsley, in the pouches and
a taller plant such as aubergine in the top of the pot.

consideration that needs to be accounted for early on in the planning of a roof garden or balcony. If you have any doubts about the weight that your roof can support, you may have to reconsider your vegetable empire and satisfy your desires by growing just a few salads and other vegetables in smaller containers and ringing the changes, when each container has been harvested. This can require a lot of forward planning as there always have to be several pots waiting in the wings.

what to choose

Containers come in all materials, sizes and shapes, so it is possible to use them for artistic effects as well as productive sites for vegetables. Some are even fitted with castors so they can be moved around easily, even when planted.

Terracotta, provided it is guaranteed to be frost-proof, is always attractive. On rooftops and balconies where weight is a consideration, plastic terracotta look-alikes are the more sensible. Traditional terracotta offers warm colours, which provide a good decorative background for vegetables. It comes in a wide range of shapes and sizes, from flowerpots to large troughs. Special pots, such as strawberry pots, can be used for other plants, such as parsley and thyme.

Galvanized iron containers bring a modern look to the vegetable garden and come in a range of shapes and sizes. If they don't come with drainage holes, either drill some across the base or add a good layer of drainage materials to the container before adding soil (see page 46 for further details).

Recycled containers. For a more quirky look, recycle large, brightly coloured olive cans or plant up a row of plastic buckets in jazzy colours. Old-fashioned butler's sinks make good containers but they are heavy. Even elegantly weathered stone urns can be pressed into service.

GARDENER'S TIP

Thuggish plants such as mint are made for containers. Their vigour is confined and you won't waste space on them, nor energy, attempting to dig them up, although growing three mints in one container is probably a bit ambitious. Peppermint, spearmint and variegated applemint offer varying flavours and attractive leaf and stem colour. For more handsome plants, grow them in separate containers.

ABOVE A child's wooden wheelbarrow has a second lease of life as a container for a number of pots of herbs. Line the base with plastic to protect it from water or place a plastic container in its base as a reservoir.

planting up a container

The minimum size of pot for growing individual vegetables is a 25 cm (10 in) pot where there is a depth of soil not less than 20 cm (8 in). Most pots have drainage holes but some will need to have holes drilled in their bases.

1 First, put in place a drainage layer so that the plants are not growing in waterlogged soil. Gravel or a layer of old terracotta pot shards are the most suitable materials or you can use crumbled pieces of polystyrene packaging. Place a large piece of pot shard or other drainage materials over the drainage holes to prevent compost washing out each time you water the containers.

2 Fill the container with a lightweight, soilless compost, adding water-retaining gel or granules.

3 If the plant is tall and will need support, add canes or trellis, depending on the size of container and the type of plants, at the time of planting, rather than later in the plant's development to prevent damaging roots.

4 Water the compost well and allow it to settle before adding more, if necessary.

5 Make planting holes large enough to take the rootball of the plants, water them in well and firm them in, taking care not to damage the roots.

ABOVE Small containers are ideal for herbs destined for a quick or short-term use. For a uniform look, apply a coat of white paint to terracotta and plastic pots.

RIGHT Deep, old-fashioned ceramic sinks make useful, small-space containers for cut-and-come-again lettuce mixes.

ABOVE *Deep and colourful, former vegetable oil drums are cleaned and recycled to provide ample space for a variety of vegetables and herbs.*

Water container-grown vegetables and fruit every day, and more frequently during dry, hot conditions. Avoid splashing water onto the leaves or flushing compost from the surface of the planting. If possible, place pots on plant saucers to hold surplus water as a reservoir for the plants and to avoid spillage and waste.

GROWING POTATOES IN A BARREL

In a small garden, try growing potatoes in a barrel or rubbish bin. Drill holes in the base and add pot shards and gravel for drainage.

1 Add a layer of garden compost and loam-based compost about 10 cm (4 in) deep.

2 Place four or five seed potatoes on top, then add another layer of soil. In a few weeks shoots will appear.

3 Once these shoots are 15–20 cm (6–8 in) tall, add more soil so that just their tips show. Water well and continue to cover the growing shoots each time they reach 15 cm (6 in) above the soil.

4 Once the soil has reached the top of the bin allow the shoots to grow. Harvest the potatoes after flowering.

window boxes, grow-bags and hanging baskets

EVEN IF YOU HAVE NO ACTUAL GARDEN, YOU CAN STILL GROW FRESH HERBS AND
VEGETABLES IN BASKETS, BOXES AND GROW-BAGS, EVEN IF THE RANGE AND QUANTITY
WILL BE LIMITED. THESE CONTAINERS CAN BE DRAFTED IN TO GROW YOUR PARTICULAR
MUST-HAVE FRESH FOOD CHOICES, SUCH AS BASIL, TUMBLING TRUSSES OF CHERRY
TOMATOES, PEPPERS, THYME AND STRAWBERRIES.

window boxes

Space is restricted in these shallow containers but they
will suit salad crops such as radishes and lettuces, which
have shallow roots. Many herbs, such as chives, marjoram,
parsley, thyme and sage, will also grow well in window
boxes. Plant them towards the front of the box and set
small tomatoes and peppers at the back of the box.
Brighten the whole effect with nasturtiums which will
also provide spicy leaves and flowers for your salads.

grow-bags

Grow-bags may not be the most stylish of containers but
they are extremely useful for large vegetables that crop
over a long period, such as tomatoes, peppers, courgettes,
cucumbers, lettuces and aubergines. They consist of
water-tight plastic bags, filled with a peat or non-peat
compost with added fertilizer.

RIGHT Tomato 'Tumbler' produces prolific trusses of luscious,
deep red cherry-type tomatoes on stems that trail over the edge
of containers such as hanging baskets and windowboxes.

To plant them up, you need to cut out sections of the plastic on the top of the bag to make a series of holes. Then set the plants into the compost through the holes. It is best to position grow-bags on a level surface, such as a patio, against a sunny wall in a sheltered site. Keep the compost moist because if it is allowed to dry out it will be difficult to re-wet.

Plants such as tomatoes and peppers will need a support system. There are several available commercially, and you can also make your own support systems using canes (see page 50).

(see page 50).

planting a hanging basket

Before you plant up the basket, check that the site that you have in mind for it is sufficiently strong and attach secure brackets that will support the quite considerable weight of plants and soil. Ensure the basket won't overhang the balcony, as dripping water from baskets will be annoying to neighbours below. Also make sure it isn't in a position where it will be inconvenient for you to reach or where you will constantly be hitting your head on it!

1 Stand the basket on a large upturned pot and line the inside of the basket with a home-made liner made from black plastic. Alternatively, use one of the many commercially available basket liners made from pressed peat or reconstituted wool shoddy.

2 Mix some compost with water-retaining gel crystals and add to the basket in layers. As you go, make small holes in the basket lining to push seedlings through, to give the planting a full and layered effect.

3 Gradually fill and plant up the sides of the basket until you put in place the plants in the top. Top up with compost, firm lightly and water well.

ABOVE Runner beans in hanging baskets will not grow to the same height as those in the ground, but will nonetheless produce a reasonable crop of fresh beans.

SUPPORT FOR GROW-BAGS

If you are growing tomatoes in grow-bags they will need to be supported as they grow, especially when they have heavy trusses of fruit. It is simple to make your own supports using bamboo canes. As the plants grow, tie stems and trusses to the canes and wires.

1 Place the grow-bag on the ground. Push a cane through each of the rectangles cut in the plastic into the ground.

2 Strengthen with wire or string wound round canes and running between each one.

ABOVE *If a window box overhangs a balcony or juts out from a window it must be firmly fixed to railings or masonry. This wooden planter provides a lightweight cover for an inner plastic container.*

RIGHT *Site the hanging basket in a sunny position, sheltered from winds. Make sure that the bracket is securely fixed and that the basket is accessible for you to water and for harvesting.*

watering tips

Regular watering of windowboxes, grow-bags and hanging baskets is crucial for the survival of the plants. Take care not to splash the foliage of plants. Watering hanging baskets requires extra care to avoid flushing out compost and exposing the roots. If possible, use a hanging basket with a hoist so you can lower it when you provide water to see where the water is flowing and control the amount. Alternatively, use a ladder or stand on a kitchen stool, so the basket is at eye-level or you are above it to see where the water flows.

chapter four:

choosing vegetable varieties

Leaf vegetables
Flower and fruiting vegetables
Gourds
Onion family
Pods and kernels
Roots, stems and bulbs
Herbs and flowers

4

growing vegetables

GROWING YOUR OWN VEGETABLES IS ONE OF GARDENING'S MOST REWARDING ASPECTS. IN LIMITED SPACES IT IS BEST TO GROW THE VEGETABLES THAT YOU ENJOY MOST. TRY OUT NEW VARIETIES BUT GIVE ROOM TO THOSE THAT OFFER THE BONUS OF COLOURFUL LEAVES, FLOWERS AND LUSCIOUS HARVESTS.

choosing vegetable varieties

IN A GARDEN WHERE SPACE IS LIMITED, YOU NEED TO CHOOSE THE VARIETIES

CAREFULLY, OPTING FOR ONES WITH COMPACT GROWING HABITS, ATTRACTIVE FOLIAGE

AND PLENTIFUL CROPS.

In a garden where space is limited, vegetables that take up large areas of the plot are on the transfer list. Cabbages, cauliflowers and Brussels sprouts belong to a group of vegetables known collectively as brassicas and are on my list of vegetables to avoid in small-space growing. They take up so much room with their large leaves and are hungry feeders. In my opinion, although fresh is best, there are other vegetables that have priority over them. Nonetheless, there are one or two brassicas that I will recommend as being suitable for the city kitchen garden, mainly because their ornamental and eating qualities outweigh the disadvantages of their size (see Curly kale on page 57, Sprouting broccoli on page 60, Kohlrabi on page 71 and Turnip on page 72).

LEFT Brassicas are space- and nutrient-hungry plants. However, this attractive, dark-leaved kale, 'Nero di Toscana' grows well in containers and looks good in mixed borders.

leaf vegetables

Lettuce

High on my list of preferences for the small garden are salads and to satisfy my love of variety in salads there is a wide choice of lettuces as well as of salad leaf collections.

Lettuce (*Lactuca sativa*), the staple of most green salads, is the dominant leaf in these salad selections, but it comes in a range of leaf sizes, shapes, textures, colours and crunch. Lettuces are divided into different types according to the shape of their head and by season. The groups are iceberg, butterhead, crisphead and cos types and over-wintering lettuces. There is also a group of lettuces known as loose leaf, cut-and-come-again, and these special types are the basis for many of the salad selections available.

Many of the small lettuces such as 'Buttercrunch', 'Tom Thumb' and 'Little Gem' have very small compact heads and are ideal for window boxes and other containers. They can be very closely planted (15–20 cm/6–8 in apart) and will still provide tasty, leafy produce.

You can sow lettuce direct into cells or modules or direct into the growing site. In rows they should be sown to a depth of 1 cm (½ in). They need regular watering once the seedlings are established, particularly in the week before harvesting. Butterheads take ten weeks to harvest, crisphead and cos types are ready at 14 weeks.

Choices: For red or mahogany-bronze leaves that look attractive in the garden and in salads try Little Leprechaun', 'Lollo Rosso', 'Marvel of Four Seasons' or 'Red Salad Bowl'. Greenest of green leaves come from 'Lollo Biondo', while 'Salad Bowl' with fresh green, heavily indented leaves is a cut-and-come-again type. Choose 'Buttercrunch', 'Tom Thumb' and 'Little Gem' for compact container growth.

Chicory

Chicory (*Cichorium intybus*) is available as forcing chicory and as a leaf chicory. Forcing chicory is blanched to a fresh spring green colour and has closely packed, upright leaves and a slightly bitter taste. Leaf chicory can be harvested as individual leaves or allowed to form a heart and harvested whole. It comes in many colourings, including red. Red chicory or radicchio adds marbled colouring to salads and looks great in winter vegetable gardens. Green leaf form or sugarloaf chicory has large lettuce-like heads and is a good over-wintering salad leaf. Chicory grows well in fertile, well-drained soil.

Sow forcing chicory in late spring or early summer direct into rows in the ground and thin to 20 cm (8 in) when the first true leaves begin to appear. Water well throughout the season. In autumn dig up the plants, harvest the foliage for use in salads, cutting them back so that about 2 cm (¾ in) of foliage is showing above the root. Cut back the roots and plant up several to a pot in moist compost. Place a second pot upside down on the rim of the first pot to act as a cover, and leave in a frost-free site for up to 12 weeks. Once the new tips are growing well they can be harvested.

Sow leaf chicory into seed trays in spring and plant out in early summer. It will be ready to harvest in summer, but you can also sow in midsummer for an autumn harvest and in late summer for growing under a cloche in winter.

Choices: Forcing chicory: 'Brussels Witloof', 'Zoom'. Leaf forms: 'Sugar Loaf', 'Palla Rossa', 'Rosso di Treviso', 'Variegata di Sottomarina'.

Salad leaf collections

These salads with foliage of differing colour, texture and taste are relatively expensive to buy from supermarkets, but can be grown and picked fresh over a long period in the year.

Among the seed selections are international salad collection packs such as English, Italian, American, French and Oriental. These combine salads that are typical for each type of cuisine and will make colourful container selections as well as look good in the ground. All have some leaves which are spicy and others which have a good background, almost bland flavour. In addition the leaves have different textures, colours and shapes, making an attractive small clump in the garden or in a container. The oriental mixture of seeds is a particularly good choice because they are extremely versatile. They can be sown in mid to late summer and used more or less as cut-and-come-again crops, or allowed to grow to full size and used as individual vegetables. They can also be over-wintered under cloches.

A French collection is likely to include herbs such as chervil, as well as leaves of lamb's lettuce or corn salad, chicory and lettuce. An Italian collection might contain salad rocket, chicory, radicchio and lettuce 'Lollo Rosso' together with the herb basil, while an Oriental collection will include a wide range of over-wintering plants such as Pak choi, purple mustard, mizuna and mibuna.

'Oriental vegetables' is the collective name given to a range of mainly cabbages or brassicas which can be grown as cut-and-come-again crops or as individual rows of single-type seed packs. They include Chinese cabbage, oriental mustard, mustard spinach (Komatsuna), Pak choi, Japanese greens (mizuna) and Japanese parsley (mitsuba). They are often sold in a mixed pack called Oriental Saladini. They grow well in sun in fertile soil and need to be well-watered. If grown as a cut-and-come-again crop you can start to pick leaves about four weeks after sowing, taking just enough to keep the plants producing more leaves for later harvests. If growing in rows as individual vegetable plants, allow 30 cm (12 in) between the rows.

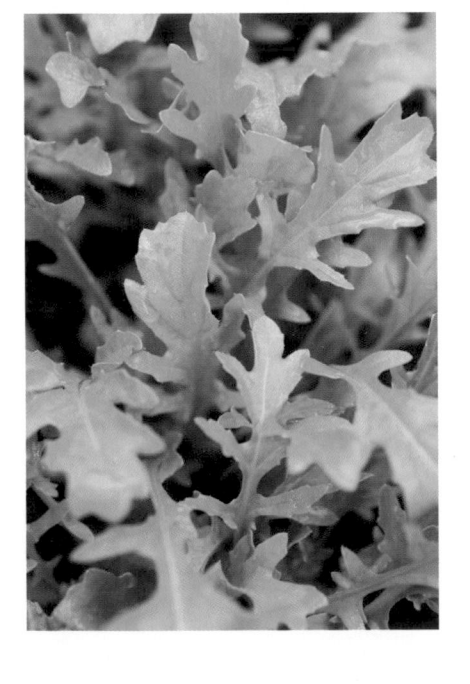

Salad rocket

Salad rocket (*Eruca sativa*) is one of the hottest of the salad leaves, offering attractive indented green leaves and white flowers, which are equally hot to taste. Wild rocket has long, deeply-cut leaves and is useful as a cut-and-come-again crop. Providing similar ferocity in a relatively small leaf is American landcress (*Barbarea montana*), which has bright yellow flowers.

Lamb's lettuce

Lamb's lettuce (*Valerianella locusta*), also known as corn salad, is a hardy annual with a dark green bitter-tasting leaf that makes a useful addition to a winter salad. It grows well in full sun or shade in fertile, moist but not waterlogged soils. Sow in spring in rows and thin to 10–15 cm (4–6 in) apart, water well and sow successively throughout the summer for later crops. Late sowings can be successfully over-wintered under cloches.

Choices: 'Verte de Cambrai', 'Vit'.

Chard

Once just available in its greenleaf form, with a striking white stem, chard (*Beta vulgaris* Cicla Group) is now available in a mixture of stem and leaf colours, adding emphasis to its ornamental qualities in the vegetable garden and in combination with flowering plants. Grow it in nitrogen-rich, fertile soil and add bulky organic matter or material from your compost bin. Sow in late spring through to midsummer for harvest during the following winter and late spring. Chard needs space so thin seedlings to 30 cm (12 in) apart. The plants need water and liquid fertilizing when young. They can be grown more closely together but this will cramp the plants and reduce the

leaf size. Chard stems and leaves are cooked separately, as the leaves need a shorter cooking time than the stems, which can be used as an asparagus substitute.

Choices: 'Burgundy Chard' has reddish stems and attractively veined leaves, 'Rhubarb Chard' has similarly deep red stems and veining. 'Bright Lights' is a seed mixture containing chard with stems in a range of shades including red, white, pink, green and yellow. The foliage is also attractive with a bronze shiny texture and strong veining. The leaves are ready 60 days from sowing. 'Lucullus' has plain white stems and white veining on the smooth foliage.

Curly kale

Curly kale (*Brassica oleracea Acephala* Group) is an appetizing winter vegetable if you pick its leaves when they are young and tender. It is one of the vegetables I consider too space-hungry for the small garden. However, there are two forms that I grow because of their wonderfully ornamental foliage. They do taste good, too, but need to be harvested when the leaves are young, which defeats my ornamental objectives somewhat!

You will need a seedling nursery bed, or container if you are growing on a balcony or patio, to hold the young plants until they are ready to plant out in late summer into their growing sites. Sow seed direct into the seed bed or a container in early spring and thin the seedlings as they mature. Water well. They are tall-growing and, if combining vegetables and flowers in a border, will suit the middle of the border. They will need supporting as the foliage rosette becomes heavy and in windy conditions may overbalance.

Choices: 'Darkibor' has deeply curled green leaves, while 'Red Bor' has similarly deeply-cut but purple-bronze leaves. 'Nero di Toscana' has an embossed, bubble-like texture to its foliage which is such a dark green that it is almost black. 'Dwarf Curled' is good for the small-space garden.

flower and fruiting vegetables

Tomatoes

Tomatoes (*Lycopersicon esculentum*) are among the sunniest fruits of the vegetable garden. Plum, beefsteak, cherry, striped, yellow, orange, red and even bronze-black are the shapes and colours available. Many seed companies have ranges of old or heritage seeds or young plants, which provide luscious fruits in even more exciting shapes and colours. With evocative names such as 'Broad Ripple Yellow Cream', 'Banana Legs' and 'Black Russian', they are frost-tender so grow them in a greenhouse, or plant outdoor varieties in the warmest site when all frost danger has passed.

There are two main types, described as bush or cordons, depending on their growth habits. Bush types need little attention, but cordons need to have side shoots taken out regularly so the plants concentrate their energies on producing a limited number of well-formed, good quality fruiting branches (trusses). When cordons have set fruit on at least 3–4 trusses, pinch out the main growing tip. If you have a wall for them to shelter against and can grow them on canes or a firm support system, cordons will provide a good crop. Some bush types that have a sprawling habit grow well in containers, hanging baskets and window boxes.

All tomatoes need full sun in a sheltered site in fertile, well-drained soil. Sow seed onto the surface of a seed tray or into a modular tray, and just cover with a little compost. Enclose the tray in a polythene bag and either place in a propagator or site where the temperature is 15–18°C (60–65°F). Prick the seedlings out when the first true leaves appear and as weather warms in early summer harden off plants during the day before planting out into the garden, or taking pots out onto a roof garden or patio. If you are growing in containers and especially in grow-bags, water regularly.

Container choices: 'Tumbler' is a popular choice for containers of all kinds and produces abundant small red fruits. 'Tornado' has abundant small red cherry-sized fruits, while 'Sun Belle' has small yellow, mini-plum shaped fruits. 'Tiny Tim' is ideal for window boxes and produces good red fruits. 'Tornado' suits containers and hanging baskets. For growing in the ground choose 'Golden Sunrise', 'San Marzano' (a plum tomato), 'Gardeners' Delight' (large trusses of small well-flavoured fruits) and 'Sweet Cherry' (masses of small red fruits).

Aubergine

The aubergine (*Solanum melongena*) needs high heat over a long period in summer if it is to fruit outdoors, otherwise it needs to be grown in a green-house. The most familiar deep purple, glossy skinned fruits are preceded by attractive mauve flowers if the temperature is at a constant 25–30°C (75–86°F). Also available is a range of unusually shaped and coloured aubergines, varying from white tennis-ball-sized fruits to long, thin, marbled-skinned ones.

Sow seed in spring into trays in a propagator where you can achieve a temperature of 15–21°C (58–70°F). Pot on when the seedlings are large enough to handle and harden off before planting outside. They need to be in full sun in a sheltered site in a well-drained, fertile soil. If growing in containers and grow-bags, keep the plants well watered and use a liquid fertilizer. Stake the plants with cane supports.

When the flowers bloom spray with a fine water mister to increase pollination and nip off side shoots when up to six fruits have formed on the plant. Harvest fruits in late summer.

Choices: 'Mini Bambino' is a short plant that produces mini-aubergines that can be cooked and served whole. 'Long Purple' and 'Black Enorma' produce large fruits. 'Red Egg' is a new offering with bright red fruits that grows well in containers. 'Chinese Ancestors' is a new collection of aubergines in different shapes and colours, including white, purple and green, in long, round and standard shapes. 'Mr Stripey' has a marbled white and purple skin, while 'Kermit' is a new white-skinned, apple-shaped aubergine. 'Bonica' produces early fruits.

Sprouting broccoli

Sprouting broccoli (*Brassica oleracea Italica Group*) is another of the space-hungry brassicas that I like to give garden room to because they are attractive and good value in terms of taste and timing. There are two forms, both with green leaves but having purple or green flowers, which are the sprouting shoots that are harvested.

You will need a space to house the seedlings over the spring and early summer until transplanting to their final growing positions. Sow seeds into rows in a seedbed and thin to 15 cm (6 in) apart. Transplant to the final growing site in midsummer with 68–75 cm (27–30 in) between plants and between rows. Sprouting broccoli needs a sunny position in

deep, free-draining but moist soil. Water well and regularly.

Sprouting broccoli will provide a regular harvest through the late winter and into early spring. Plants may need staking or earthing up at the roots to provide extra stability. Remove the central shoot and pick the prolific purple or green flowering shoots as they appear. Keep cutting to ensure regular shoot production.

Choices: 'Early Purple Sprouting' is ready in late winter; 'Early White Sprouting' in early spring. Choose 'Red Arrow' for purple spears over a long period.

Peppers

Peppers (*Capsicum annuum*), often called sweet bell or wax peppers, with brightly coloured bell-shaped fruits in yellow, green, red and purple, need greenhouse protection in cold temperate climates, but can be planted out into the sunniest, most sheltered position in the garden or patio in summer. Sow two seeds per pot or cell, if using modular seed trays, in early spring and provide a temperature of 21°C (70°F). As the seedlings germinate and establish, reduce the heat to 12–15°C (55–60°F). Transplant them when their first flowers appear and, after

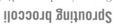

hardening off, grow in grow-bags or other containers. Provide liquid fertilizer and water the plants well if in containers. The fruits are ready to harvest when green, but if you leave them on the plants they will ripen over a three-week period to red, yellow or purple depending on variety.

Choices: 'Big Banana' has long red fruits, 'Sweet Chocolate' has dark, almost black-skinned fruit. Mixed selections of yellow, orange, green, red and black peppers are also available.

gourds

Within this group of large fruits are many of my favourite vegetables including courgettes (immature marrows), squash and pumpkins. While courgettes, pumpkins and squash are the fruits of large space-demanding, sprawling plants, I include them in the small urban garden because they are rewarding in terms of ornament and use, as well as nutrition and kitchen use. And as they have a vining, climbing habit you can grow them in a more limited space than you might at first think possible.

Courgette

Courgette (*Cucurbita pepo*) or zucchini are the immature fruits of the marrow and grow well in fertile, moist soils. If grown in containers provide them with regular and copious amounts of water as they are thirsty plants. Their flowers are also edible and look attractive served with mini-courgettes attached. Pick the courgettes regularly when they are about 10–15 cm (4–6 in) long. If you leave them on the plant the crop numbers will reduce and individual fruits will be large and marrow-like.

Choices: 'Black Forest' is a climbing variety that is useful for covering trellis and arches and for small-space growing. 'Ambassador' is also a compact plant and for a colourful crop outdoors and in the kitchen, 'Jemmer', 'Gold Rush' and 'Taxi' are yellow-skinned courgettes.

Either sow seed in early spring in a heated propagator or two or three seeds directly into the ground once all frost danger is over. If direct sowing into the ground cover the sowing site with a mini-cloche, such as a plastic bottle with its bottom removed. This will act as a mini-greenhouse and warm the soil around the germinating seedling. When the seedlings have germinated, thin them to leave just one seedling.

Pumpkin and Squash

Pumpkin (*Cucurbita maxima*) and squash (*Cucurbita moschata*) are annual vining plants that will rush along the ground or rise, like jungle creatures, up supports to reach the sunshine. If you do grow them over supports make sure they are strong as these fruits and foliage are very weighty. Most pumpkins are too large for the small garden but there are several that produce prolific small fruits that provide meals in themselves and can be very decorative in the vegetable garden. Squash are nutty textured

and come in all shapes and sizes. Like pumpkin, they keep well over the winter if cured in the sun after harvest and stored in a dry frost-free site until ready for use. Sowing is as for courgettes. In containers they need to be well watered at the base of the plant.

Choices: 'Jack be Little' and 'Baby Bear' are small pumpkins, the former just fitting into the palm of your hand. 'Crown Prince', with a bluish skin, is a very densely textured

pumpkin, which is perfect for savoury dishes; it also looks attractive in the garden.

In the squash family there are many small and attractive fruits including 'Butternut', 'Kabocha', 'Table Ace' and 'Sweet Dumpling'.

onion family

Leeks

Leeks (*Allium porrum*) are one of the staples of the autumn and winter kitchen garden, providing pungent onion flavour and attractive strappy foliage in grey and silvery tones. In addition, if your soil is heavy the leek's root system will help to improve soil structure. They do well in open sites in average garden soil. Sow seed directly into a seed bed in spring, 2.5 cm (1 in) deep and 15 cm (6 in) apart.

When the seedlings are about as thick as your little finger and 20 cm (8 in) tall, usually about 12 weeks after sowing, transplant them into their growing site. Before lifting, water them well and make planting holes 15–20 cm (6–8 in) deep and 15 cm (6 in) apart. Use a trowel to lift the young plants, and trim the leaves a little and drop them into individual planting holes. Swirl water into the planting hole but don't back

fill with soil. Keep the row weed-free and water regularly. Harvest by lifting the plants with a fork.

Choices: 'Carentan' and 'Natan' produce sturdy white stems and have attractive grey-green foliage. 'King Richard' has a long white shaft and is a good choice for growing at a closer spacing to produce mini-leeks. 'Musselburgh' is a popular old variety.

Onions

Onions (*Allium cepa*) are grown for their tasty swollen bulbs and can be raised from specially prepared small onions called onion sets, or from seed. If you are growing vegetables in a small space and don't have a greenhouse or room for a seedbed, then the solution is to grow onions from sets.

There are two disadvantages to growing from sets. You may not have the same range of varieties available as sets as there are seeds. Onions grown from sets tend to run to flower or 'bolt', so buy sets that are labelled as 'heat-treated'.

Onions need well-drained, fertile soil in a sunny open site. Plant sets into the ground in autumn or from late winter right the way through to mid-spring, in rows, just covering them with soil so that the tips just show above the soil surface. They should be 5 cm (2 in) apart. If you have the space and facilities to grow from seed, sow indoors in winter and provide temperatures of 10–16°C (50–60°F). After hardening off the seedlings, plant them out into their growing site in spring. Spring, salad or bunching onions can be sown in succession through the growing season in spring and summer. They can be sown direct into the ground and thinned to 2.5 cm (1 in).

Choices: 'Ailsa Craig' produces mild-flavoured bulbs, but is not a good keeping onion. 'Autumn Gold' is a good keeper. 'New Fen Globe' is available in heat-treated sets. For attractive colour and strong flavour, the red onion 'Red Baron' is a good keeping onion. 'White Lisbon' and 'White Lisbon Winter Hardy' are two bunching onions that will give you salad material right throughout the year.

pods and kernels

Beans

There are several species of bean that provide ornamental flowers, well-coloured tasty pods or beans that will suit small spaces and containers.

Runner beans and some French or haricot beans are climbing plants that will provide good cover on trellises or can be used as screens on patios.

Runner beans

Runner beans (*Phaseolus coccineus*) will do best in sites that have been well-prepared in the autumn and winter before planting in spring. They grow best in a warm sheltered site with a little shade. They are frost tender so should either be sown indoors and transplanted when all frost danger is past, or sown direct into the growing site in late spring or early summer when the soil temperature has risen to about 10°C (50°F).

Runner beans need supporting and the traditional way to do this is with canes and twine. Either make a circular wigwam of canes, tied at the top like a teepee, or have a double row of canes tied to each other at the top, and linked along the whole row by canes laid across the V-shaped tops of the cane rows. You can also set the canes into the ground as uprights and secure bean or pea netting to them or use twine to give the beans a foothold.

Pinch out the tops of the bean plants when they reach the top of the canes. Water well and regularly, particularly when in flower. Sometimes a fine spray on the flowers aids pollination if bees are in short supply or the flowers are infested with pollen beetles, which deter bees. Harvest regularly from midsummer to keep pod production going.

Choices: 'Flamenco' and 'Relay' have flowers in three colours – white, red and bi-colour – and 'Flamenco' is a low-growing compact plant that will suit containers. 'White Lady' has plain white flowers and produces long, smooth, stringless pods. 'Painted Lady' is an old variety with white and red bi-coloured flowers and well-flavoured pods. 'Prize winner', 'Lady Di' and 'Galaxy' are among the red-flowered varieties. 'Hestia' is a dwarf runner bean with a good flavour, producing long, straight, stringless pods. It has bi-coloured flowers and, like all runner beans, is attractive in containers and in the small vegetable garden.

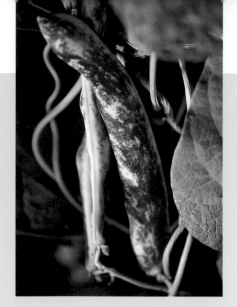

French beans

French beans (*Phaseolus vulgaris*), also known as dwarf and snap beans, are usually small and bushy although there are some climbing varieties. Their pods are green, purple or yellow. They are frost tender so should either be started early indoors and transplanted outside when all danger of frost has past or sown direct outside when soil temperature is around 13°C (56°F). From late spring through to midsummer you can sow outdoors to provide a successional crop. Sow seeds 3 cm (1 in) deep in soil and leave 23 cm (9 in) between plants. They grow best in full sun in a fertile, slightly acid soil in a sheltered position and need regular watering, particularly when in flower.

Choices: Climbing forms include 'Barlotta Lingua di Fuoco' which has attractively pink-and-cream marbled skins on pods and on the beans, which can be used as haricots towards the end of the growing season. 'Corona d'Oro' is a yellow-podded climber, 'Cosse Violette' has purple pods and 'Kentucky Blue' produces long pods ready to pick 8–9 weeks after sowing. The ultimate in colour and taste comes from the lablab or hyacinth bean (Dolichos lablab) 'Ruby Moon', which has flat purple pods and flowers.

For bush or dwarf beans, 'Sungold' is a golden yellow pod on a compact bushy plant, 'Royalty' and 'Purple Teepe' are purple-podded bush beans, while 'Aramis' and 'Maxi' are prolific green-podded bush beans.

Peas

Peas (*Pisum sativum*) are scrambling annuals in two forms — as shelling peas, which are taken out of the pods after harvest, and as pod or mangetout peas, where the whole pod and the immature peas within it are eaten. You can sow to over-winter for harvesting in late spring, but in a small space it is simpler to sow direct into the ground or containers in spring. They need well-watered, fertile, well-prepared soil and will tolerate some shade but need to be supported early on. A twiggy framework of hazel pea-sticks is useful once the peas are growing well, forming a decorative low hedge or screen. Holly leaves along the line of the sowing may put off mice and wire netting tunnels hooped over seedlings will deter birds.

Choices: Mangetout or snap peas: 'Sugar Snap', 'Oregon Sugar Pod' and 'Ambrosia' will provide tender and juicy pods over a long period.

Early garden or pod peas: 'Tafila' is one of the earliest to crop and has semi-leafless stems. 'Kelvedon Wonder', 'Early Onward' and 'Daybreak' are good prolific early peas, while for a maincrop choose 'Alderman'. 'Hurst Green Shaft' and 'Onward' produce pods packed with plump peas. For extra ornamental value, grow the pink-red flowered 'Yuhsaya'.

Broad beans

Broad beans (*Vicia faba*) are very hardy and can be sown in late autumn/early winter to over-winter and crop from early summer. They grow well in heavy but not water-logged soil in sun. Sow in double rows 20 cm (8 in) apart. A system of posts with string attached will keep plants upright and stop them being toppled in windy conditions. They can also be sown in late winter to provide a crop in summer. Pinch out the growing tips once the first flowers have set.

Choices: 'Aquadulce' is an old variety that crops well from early winter sowing. 'Green Windsor' has short pods with fewer beans but is well-flavoured. 'Red Epicure' has startling red beans inside the green pod. 'The Sutton' is a dwarf bush form with good yields. Broad beans have white flowers, but heritage seed with crimson flowers is available from specialist seed suppliers

Sweetcorn

Sweetcorn (*Zea mays*) or corn on the cob provides sweet kernels in regimented rows along its length. Yellow or creamy-white are the usual colours, but there are also some colourful varieties. Some are strictly ornamental while others have an excellent flavour as well.

Sweetcorn is a tall plant and as it is wind-pollinated it is best to grow it in blocks so plants can cross-pollinate. Although it needs wind for pollination, it should be grown in a relatively sheltered position. Earthing up the soil around the plant's roots will help keep it stable in unsheltered sites. Grow in full sun in a free-draining but moisture-retentive, fertile, slightly acid soil. It needs warmth to germinate and soil temperatures above 10°C (50°F).

Sow indoors, two to three seeds per pot, in late spring at a temperature of 13°C (55°F). Once the seedlings are growing remove all but the strongest one from the pot.

Harden off and plant out when all frost danger is past. Plants need to be about 35 cm (14 in) apart, but can be more closely planted in containers. Water regularly, especially when in flower. Once the silks or tassels turn brown they are ready to harvest.

Choices: New varieties of sweetcorn, bred for their sweetness, are often described as Supersweet. If you grow them with older varieties, they are likely to cross-pollinate each other, resulting in a loss of sweetness in the newer varieties. It's therefore best to grow the different types quite separate from each other. 'Sweet Nugget' is a supersweet variety with a deep yellow, long cob. 'Sunrise' is a compact plant that can be closely planted. 'Honey and Cream' has white and yellow kernels on the cob but is tall growing. 'Blue Jade' produces small cobs with blue kernels; it has a dwarf, bushy shape and suits containers or small spaces.

BABY VEGETABLES

Close spacing some vegetable varieties results in mini-versions of the mature form, packed full of flavour and offering 'designer' vegetables on a small-scale. Also known as mini-vegetables or high-density vegetables, many have been bred to perform well at closer spacing than traditional vegetables. They are high-yielding, making them a perfect choice for small-space gardening. Cabbages and cauliflowers produce mini-heads if grown to a spacing of 10 cm (4 in) and 15 cm (6 in) respectively, while leeks will be pencil-thin and just as tasty as full-size leeks if spaced to 1 cm (½ in). In some cases you will need to check seed catalogues to see which varieties are recommended for growing as baby vegetables.

roots, stems and bulbs

Potatoes

Potatoes (*Solanum tuberosum*) may seem to be too space-hungry for the small garden, but the taste of home-grown potatoes outweighs that caveat. There are special varieties bred for close growing and methods of growing in containers which, although they won't yield an over-abundant crop, will produce enough for the small-space gardener to enjoy (see page 47). Seed merchants and garden centres are recognizing this fact and selling packs of smaller quantities of seed potatoes. There are also numerous old varieties sold described as heritage varieties which have been worked on to improve their disease- and pest-resistance. They offer good taste and in many cases well-coloured skins for salads as well as swirls of colour within the potato flesh itself.

If you have the space, grow varieties from the three main harvests: early potatoes (ready for harvest about 8–10 weeks after planting), second early (ready from mid to late summer), as well as a late or main crop potato. Potatoes are susceptible to many diseases so buy certified virus-free seed potatoes and choose varieties that are more disease-resistant. Early crops are useful as they are harvested before slugs and wireworms can damage them.

Seed potatoes have to be prepared to make them shoot before planting out. Egg boxes make suitable containers to stand seed potatoes or tubers in. Keep the potatoes in a cool, frost-free and light site for about six weeks while they 'chit' or send out small shoots. Plant the tubers into trenches in the well-drained, fertile soil in a sunny site. Early varieties go in from early to mid-spring, with main crops planted from mid- to late spring. Keep the tubers about 30 cm (12 in) apart and main crops 38 cm (15 in) apart with 50–75 cm (20–30 in) between rows, with early potatoes closer together than the main crop varieties. Protect the rows with a cover of horticultural fleece, especially if frosts are forecast. When shoots appear above ground, fork up the soil in the rows to make a ridge above the potatoes to protect them from frosts and to keep them out of the light. If they have contact with light they will turn green and become poisonous. Water the soil around the plants well in dry weather.

Many varieties have attractive flowers and these are a useful indicator of when to harvest. Early potatoes are ready to harvest when the flowers are opening on the stems (about 9–10 weeks from planting), while main crops are left in the ground until autumn when the flowering stems die down. Dig them up, allow to dry off and store in the dark in a cool, frost-free site. Early potatoes are thin-skinned and delicious eaten soon after harvest. They are not suitable for storing. Second earlies and main crop are larger and suitable for storing.

Choices: 'Dunluce' is an extra early potato with compact growth and suits forcing in pots in a greenhouse or in containers. 'Foremost' is a first early which also has compact growth and is usually left untouched by slugs. 'Kestrel' is a second early with good resistance to slugs. 'Valor' is a main crop potato which is compact and resistant to tuber blight with good tolerance of eelworm. 'Mimi' is a new cherry-sized, red-skinned punnet potato. It is lifted early and treated as an early crop, but can be planted closer than traditional early potatoes.

Radishes

Radishes (*Raphanus sativus*), grown for their spicy and colourful swollen roots, come in many shapes, sizes and colours. Salad radishes are fast-growing and ready to harvest four weeks after sowing; winter varieties take longer to mature. Radishes need a light, well-drained but moist and well-prepared soil. Summer-sown radishes need a little shade, so are useful for intercropping.

Sow small amounts of radish seed at regular intervals in short rows and thin to 2.5 cm (1 in) between plants. Winter radishes need up to 15 cm (6 in) between plants. They should be sown during summer for autumn and winter harvests, while salad radishes can be sown from early spring through to autumn.

Choices: 'Cherry Belle', 'French Breakfast' and 'Scarlet Globe' are good salad radishes, while 'China Rose', with white flesh, and 'Mantanghong', with crimson flesh, are good winter varieties.

Carrots

Carrots (*Daucus carota*) can be sown in succession to provide harvests at different times during the year. Traditionally grown for their long, fat roots, there are also short-rooted varieties which are useful for container growing or for heavy soils. Carrots need full sun in a well-prepared site and plenty of water. Short-rooted varieties take only 15 weeks to mature, so even though you won't have the traditional carrot shape you will have several harvests of sweet and succulent stump-rooted carrots.

Sow seed at the beginning of spring into shallow rows 12 mm (½ in) deep and 15 cm (6 in) apart. Carrot seed is fine, and pelleted or coated seeds are easier to sow. Cover with soil and water well. Protect the row with a cloche if sowing early in spring until the plants are growing well. Carrot fly is a serious pest (see page 27).

Choices: 'Amsterdam Forcing' matures early, 'Redca' is suitable on shallow soils, 'Early Market' is a short-rooted carrot with good flavour and colour, 'Early Nantes' is a good carrot for the small garden and 'Parmex' and 'Parabell' are two varieties with almost round roots. 'Flyaway' is a good main crop, long-rooted carrot with resistance to carrot fly.

Kohlrabi

Kohlrabi (*Brassica oleracea Gongylodes* Group) is a swollen stem which can be grated raw into salads or cooked and served whole or sliced. It is available in green and purple forms, making it an ornamental as well as a productive vegetable.

Kohlrabi needs a sunny site in a well-drained, fertile soil. It can be grown as a mini-vegetable and suits container growing well. It needs regular watering otherwise the centre becomes woody. Apply a high-nitrogen fertilizer during the growing season. If growing in containers, apply a general fertilizer every three weeks.

Sow into the ground in late winter but protect tender seedlings with cloches. Continue to sow through the spring and summer to keep a succession of plants going. You can also sow in autumn for a later harvest, but this sowing will need the protection of cloches. Harvest from midsummer onwards when the kohlrabi is well-rounded and about the size of a tennis ball.

Choices: 'Green Delicacy' and 'Purple Delicacy' offer green and purple skins and good leaf colourings as well.

Beetroot

Beetroot (*Beta vulgaris*) provides young leaves that spice up salads in terms of colour and taste, as well as its swollen root which is delicious eaten as a hot vegetable or pickled. There are many shapes, ranging from round, globe shapes to long, thin tapering roots. New 'monogerm' varieties can be sown more closely spaced as they don't need to be thinned and are ideal for small-space growing.

Beetroot needs a light, well-drained and well-prepared soil. Soak seeds for up to an hour to reduce effects of the natural germination inhibitor they contain. Non-monogerm seed is a small beetroot fruit containing up to three seeds, so if all three germinate thin them eventually to a distance of 10 cm (4 in). Sow seed in mid-spring into rows, if necessary protecting with cloches to warm up the soil. Thin the seedlings, as necessary, and mulch the row to conserve water and to reduce weeds.

Choices: For baby beets and to avoid the task of thinning, use a monogerm variety such as 'Monogram', 'Moneta', and 'Monopoly'. Beetroot can bolt, so choose varieties described as bolt-resistant such as 'Boltardy', 'Regala' (good for container growing) and 'Detroit 6 Rubidus'. For unusual coloured beets choose Burpee's 'Golden' with yellow flesh and 'Chioggia Pink' with rings of pink and white flesh, which fade on cooking.

Parsnip

Parsnip (*Pastinaca sativa*) is a winter-hardy root vegetable which grows best in full sun in a light soil. If your soil is heavy or you are growing in containers, use one of the stump-rooted varieties. Sow seed direct into the growing site from late winter through to early spring. Parsnips should always be sown direct as they dislike root disturbance. Thin the seedlings out to about 15 cm (6 in) between plants. Water regularly and

keep the site weed-free. Harvest parsnips from mid-autumn onwards through the winter.

Choices: Parsnips tend to get a disease called canker, so choose resistant varieties such as 'Avonresister' which also produces small roots, so is suited to small-space and container growing.

Turnip

Turnip (*Brassica rapa*) is a fast-growing root vegetable that can be used raw in salads or cooked. It grows well in alkaline, well-drained soil in a sunny open site that was manured for the previous crop grown on the site. Sow direct outdoors in early spring and late summer, avoiding sowing in early or midsummer as hot weather induces turnips to bolt. Protect early sown seedlings with cloches if necessary. Thin first sowings to 12 cm (5 in) just as the seedlings establish and later sowings to 23 cm (9 in). Check for flea beetles and water well in dry weather, keep weed-free and harvest early sowings from late spring into early summer and later or maincrop sowings from mid-autumn. You can leave them in the ground over winter, but they will need some protection. A mulch of straw is probably suitable.

Choices: 'Golden Ball' has yellow flesh and matures in about 60 days from a spring sowing. 'Milan Purple Top' is a flattened root which matures quickly and is good for early sowing. 'Veitch's Red Globe' has dark red skin and white flesh and is also suitable for an early sowing. Use its leaves as a spinach substitute. 'Green Top Stone' can be sown late in autumn for winter use.

herbs and flowers

Culinary herbs such as thyme (*Thymus* spp.), rosemary (*Rosmarinus officinalis*), parsley (*Petroselinum crispum*), sage (*Salvia officinalis*), summer savory (*Satureja montana*), bay (*Laurus nobilis*), chives (*Allium schoenoprasum*), mint (*Mentha* spp.) and basil (*Ocimum basilicum*) are among the popular choices for kitchen gardens.

Herbs can be grown in straight rows in the garden or mixed in with the flower border and many of them grow well in containers. Rosemary and bay can be grown into standard shapes and used as formal ornamental features as well as for the kitchen. Thyme in its creeping forms suits hanging baskets and both ordinary chives and garlic chives have flowers that are pretty enough to fit into the flower border. Sage comes in a range of leaf colours and combines well with perennials. It also makes a good container plant.

BELOW *Herbs look attractive grown between the spokes of a cartwheel raised up on bricks.*

Mint, one of the natural thugs of the herb garden, spreading quickly by its vigorous root-runners, is a perfect herb to grow in containers. There are several variegated forms, including striped golden and green ginger mint, which will offer ornamental value. Mint can be cut back after flowering and one or two roots potted up and brought indoors to continue growing over the winter.

Many herbs are available from supermarkets already potted up, so if you don't have space to grow your own, buy them on a regular basis and pot them on and grow them for the short term on the patio or balcony, using them as you need them.

Edible flowers

Many herb flowers, including chives, summer savory, rosemary and basil, have wonderfully aromatic flavours and can be added to salads. Other flowers such as nasturtium (*Tropaeolum majus*), heartsease (*Viola tricolor*) and pot marigold (*Calendula officinalis*) provide colour and flavour to food. There are many garden flowers whose petals can be eaten, but unless you are sure that a plant is edible, do not eat it!

Pick the flowers early in the day and rinse them under a cold tap to dislodge any lurking insects. Dry them on absorbent paper towels and keep in the refrigerator in plastic boxes until you are ready to use them.

ABOVE *The flowers of the pot marigold are edible.*

chapter five:

choosing fruit varieties

The right rootstock
Special shapes

choosing fruit trees

Avoiding problems
Pollinators for apples
Planting fruit trees
Awaiting fruit

growing soft fruits

Choosing varieties
Practicalities

growing strawberries

The plants
Making space
Planting
Table-top system

growing shrubby fruit

Gooseberries
Redcurrants
Blackcurrants
Blueberries
Frost protection

growing cane fruits

Raspberries
Blackberries
Hybrid berries

5

growing fruit

IN A CITY KITCHEN GARDEN, A GENEROUS ORCHARD WITH NUMEROUS TREES IS
NOT POSSIBLE, BUT WITH PLANNING YOU CAN MAXIMIZE YOUR HARVEST OF
LUSCIOUS SOFT FRUITS AND JUICY TOP FRUITS. HOME-GROWN FRUIT HAS
THE EDGE IN TERMS OF SATISFACTION AND UNBEATABLE FLAVOUR.

choosing fruit varieties

SOFT FRUIT, SUCH AS STRAWBERRIES, RASPBERRIES AND BLACKBERRIES, AND TOP FRUIT,
INCLUDING APPLES, PEARS AND PEACHES, CAN BE GROWN IN THE GROUND AS WELL AS
IN CONTAINERS.

ABOVE Apples can be trained into many shapes that will add
architectural focus to the small garden and supply a good harvest
of fruit. The branches of the tree are tied onto the metal hoops of
a pre-formed globe, the upright of which is secured to the tree
trunk for support.

the right rootstock

To get the most out of your space, grow fruit trees
such as apples, pears and plums grafted onto dwarfing
root stock. They double-up as productive plants and
decorative features, such as 45 cm (18 in) or knee-high
step-over hedges, or train them into shapes against walls
or fences. Tree fruit such as apples, pears and figs will
need to be potted on from time to time into larger
containers, until finally they are in containers with a
diameter of 45 cm (18 in) and at least 45 cm (18 in)
deep.

When you order a tree check its rootstock. Apples
(*Malus sylvestris* var. *domestica*), plums (*Prunus domestica*),
pears (*Pyrus communis* var. *sativa*) and cherries (*Prunus
cerasifera* and *Prunus avium*) are grafted onto so-called
rootstocks, which control their growth rate and their
final size.

Apples Rootstocks for apples are identified with the
initial M and a number. This refers to East Malling
and Long Ashton Research Stations where the original
work on rootstocks was carried out. M9 is a dwarfing
rootstock, M26 is a semi-dwarfing rootstock used for
bush, espaliers and some upright-growing or columnar
trees. These trees are useful as screens but they can also
be grown in containers. M27 is a dwarfing rootstock,
ideal for plants grown as cordons.

SPECIAL SHAPES

There are a number of specially developed columnar shapes which are sold under a variety of trade names such as Pillarette and Minarette. These are specially suited to container growing or small-space gardens as a number of these upright trees can be grown in a small area. Some have two varieties of apples grafted onto them, offering you double the choice in a small space.

There are also a number of techniques which are used to train fruit trees into space-saving shapes. These include cordons, double cordons, fans, espaliers, pyramids, half-standards and step-overs. Two new systems where the trees are grown in V-shaped shows or trained into curved S-shapes encourage better fruit production and reduce the space needed in traditional planting systems.

Cordons are single-stemmed trees planted at a sloping angle, with their branches trained on wires. Although each plant produces less fruit, you can grow several along the edge of a path or as a hedge to enclose a garden.

Espaliers are trained so their branches grow in horizontal pairs from the main stem along wires or a wall. The main stem is upright and the trees can be taken to whatever height you wish, but need to rise in even pairs of branches.

Step-over hedges are really mini-espalier systems, with one pair of branches growing horizontally from the main stem. Their height of 30–45 cm (12–18 in) makes them a decorative as well as productive hedge for a small vegetable garden.

Pears are grown on Quince A and B rootstocks.

Plums, damsons, peaches, apricots and nectarines are on St Julien A rootstock. Pixy is a dwarfer rootstock for plums and damsons.

Cherries Tabel is a dwarfing rootstock for cherries, keeping them to a height of 1.8–2.4 m (6–8 ft).

RIGHT *Apple 'Discovery' trained into a mini-espalier system provides a seasonal display of flowers, followed by shiny fruits. At just 45 cm (18 in) high, this system described as a 'step-over' hedge, offers the twin opportunities of ornament and productivity so prized by small-space fruit growers.*

RIGHT Upright apple trees are useful in the border and are also suited to containers. Sold as 'Minarettes' or 'Pillarettes', they crop well and if grown against a wall can be netted to prevent bird damage to blossoms.

to keep the tree in good health.

Although young trees need protection from excessive wind in their early years, a good circulation of air and an open, light site will go a long way to reduce pest and disease levels. Basic hygiene, such as keeping the site clean and free of diseased leaves and fruits, helps

Control the spread of brown rot on fruit by taking off any affected fruits, otherwise this fungal condition will move through each cluster quickly (do not compost affected fruit).

Mulching to prevent soil moisture loss is also an effective and relatively simple way to control bitter pit in apples (spotting just beneath the skin of the fruit and pits on the skin surface) which is caused by calcium deficiency during times of drought.

Mulching the ground around the tree's base and feeding it with a good fertilizer or with a fish, blood and bone mix are two ways of promoting health and vigour, raising its resistance to attack.

There are also other ways in which you can control the likelihood of potential trouble.

avoiding problems

CHOOSE FRUIT TREES THAT THE GROWERS IDENTIFY AS HAVING GOOD PEST- AND DISEASE-RESISTANCE AND AVOID THOSE VARIETIES THAT COULD POSE PROBLEMS.

choosing fruit trees

pollinators for apples

Most fruit nurseries indicate suitable pollinators by number or initials. So choose trees shown in catalogues as having the same number or letter grouping. Trees from the immediate neighbouring groups can also be chosen, as they will have enough of an overlapping flowering period to pollinate each other. Some types of apple are described as poor pollinators, so you will need to grow two others from the relevant groups to keep the pollen going round for the fruit to set. In a small kitchen garden, these varieties are probably best avoided.

planting fruit trees

Once you have chosen the shape and varieties you want to grow, order the trees from specialist growers and nurseries. If you buy trees 3–4 years old, they will already be pruned into a good shape and you will only need to prune to produce fruiting branches. Bare-rooted apples are traditionally planted in late autumn to early spring, depending on soil conditions.

1 Prepare the site well by removing all perennial weeds and digging the soil to get it well aerated.

2 Make a planting hole for each of your trees, large enough to spread the roots into. The depth of the hole depends on the height of the soil mark on the stem. This enables you to keep the union (where the rootstock and grafted stem join) above soil level.

3 Knock a strong stake into the ground, so that it is firmly in place and its head is just below the first branches of the tree.

4 Fill the planting hole with the topsoil you have removed, mixed with compost and bonemeal.

5 Once the tree is in place in the planting hole, tie it to the stake. Water the tree in well after planting and all through the first spring and summer and see that they are well watered.

awaiting fruit

Young trees should not be allowed to fruit in their first year, so you will have to remove blossom in the first year after planting. This encourages the tree to put its energy into establishing good roots and a strong structure, and stimulates it to produce abundant flowers and fruit next year.

Citrus, nectarines and peaches also suit container growing in sheltered and sunny gardens and on sheltered patios. Bring citrus trees inside during winter in cold temperate climates.

Columnar trees in the Minarette and Pillarette ranges can be planted fairly close to each other at a distance of 60 cm (2 ft). They will crop when they reach a height of 1.8–2.4 m (6–8 ft).

RIGHT Citrus trees offer fragrance and ornament from their scented flowers while their glossy foliage and decorative fruits are additional attributes. They should be brought inside at the first mention of frost.

growing soft fruits

HOME-GROWN AND FRESH, SOFT FRUIT MUST SURELY BE ONE OF THE MOST DELICIOUS
AND EAGERLY AWAITED HARVESTS TO COME FROM THE KITCHEN GARDEN DURING THE
SUMMER MONTHS.

Soft fruits, including blackberries, red- and whitecurrants, gooseberries, raspberries, strawberries and many others, supply the extra ingredients that round off a summer's day meal.

Although soft fruits are usually grown in netted cages to protect them from birds, they can be just as successfully grown in smaller quantities mixed with herbs and vegetables in a potager, or even as decorative shrubs within a mixed border.

choosing varieties

There are many disease-resistant cultivars, as well as early- or late-fruiting varieties to choose.

Raspberries and blackberries Plants such as raspberries and blackberries, known as cane fruit, are suckering and rambling plants respectively. Without support they would sprawl and scramble. Give them support, and use them and their supports to make a fruitful and ornamental hedge in part of the kitchen garden or as a screen against a shed wall.

Currants are woody shrubs and can be grown in rows, mixed into a border or as centrepieces in a herb and vegetable patch.

LEFT A framework of canes supports netting to provide temporary protection for individual trees from greedy birds.

practicalities

If you are using the site as a mixed kitchen and ornamental garden, you will have prepared the soil sufficiently to support the fruit bushes' needs. In such a well-dug, well-composted site, in free-draining soil, they will have the basics necessary for good growth. You may still need to net them if birds compete with you for the harvest. If you have the space for a separate fruit cage, you can group soft fruit together, making it easier to protect the fruit from bird damage. If you cannot net the whole area, net individual plants using a temporary framework of canes to support the netting.

BELOW Red- and whitecurrants and gooseberries can be trained into half-standards, offering the small-space gardener attractive focal features and abundant fruit.

Blueberries are also woody shrubs, and need acid soil, so if you haven't the right soil conditions, grow them in ericaceous (lime-free) compost in large containers in a sheltered, but sunny site on a patio. You will need to grow two varieties to ensure pollination. In acid soil conditions they make a useful addition to a rhododendron and azalea planting. Their spring flowers are followed by fruits in summer and the attractive foliage makes a good autumnal show.

Using soft fruit ornamentally means that you are growing less for unlimited produce and more for beauty. You can only plant a few fruit bushes or canes, just sufficient to fill the space available, and you need to take extra care if you apply insecticide to the fruit bushes. The benefits of this type of double use are that you will have sufficient fruit to enjoy, and they will provide attraction with their shape, flowers and fruit.

growing strawberries

STRAWBERRIES ARE AMONG THE MOST EVOCATIVE OF SUMMER FRUITS AND, TO MY MIND,

NO KITCHEN GARDEN IS COMPLETE WITHOUT A POT OR TWO.

the plants

Strawberries are herbaceous perennials that spread by making daughter plants at the end of long runners sent out from the main plant. You can either pot up the new plants or discard them if the existing plants are providing enough fruit.

Strawberries grow to form ground-covering mounds and can be used to make informal edging rows or ground cover in a mixed border.

making space

In conventional gardens strawberries take up a great deal of ground space, but the inventive small-space grower can grow them in pots. Strawberries can also be grown in specially made barrels or terracotta planters. The latest method, known as the table-top method, is on raised strawberry platforms in grow-bags (see box, opposite) or wide window box-style containers. Instead of growing strawberries in rows, plant them

GARDENER'S TIP

Alpine strawberries (*Fragaria vesca*), with smaller leaves and more compact growth, make neat edges for borders and paths and provide sweeter fruits.

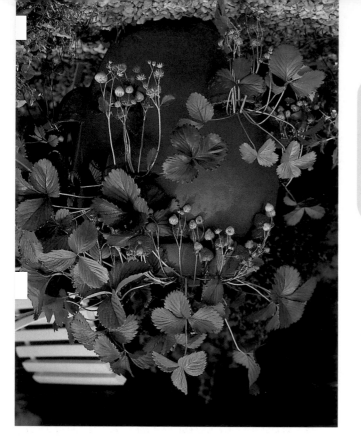

on either side of a path through the kitchen garden. Position them at least 30 cm (12 in) away from the edge of the bed. In summer when they flower and fruits begin to form, put in place a layer of straw around the plants to keep the fruits off the soil and free from dirt in wet conditions.

BELOW Specially shaped terracotta pots with scooped-out planting pouches are a popular choice for growing strawberries in limited spaces. Take care when watering not to flush out compost from the top or pouches.

planting

Water newly bought strawberry plants or soak bare-rooted plants in water before planting, but get them into their growing site as soon as possible. Set the plants about 30 cm (12 in) apart and plant them into a 15 cm (6 in) planting hole. Make sure there is space in the hole for the roots to fit. Weed around the plants regularly.

Strawberries, especially alpine strawberries, can also be grown in special tower containers on patios, and more for ornament than serious fruit, in hanging baskets. Many delicious varieties are available, including 'Cambridge Favourite', 'Elsanta' and 'Cambridge Late Pine', as well as more ornamental forms including a pink flowered strawberry, Fragaria 'Pink Panda' and a variegated leaf form, Fragaria variegata.

RIGHT *Alpine strawberries fruit over a long period from late summer through to late autumn. The sweet, fragrant fruits are smaller than other varieties, and they are ideal for growing as informal edges for borders or as productive groundcover.*

TABLE-TOP SYSTEM

Commercial strawberry growers have developed a raised system for growing strawberries en masse. There are kits available for home use. The idea is to grow the fruits at table height so they are easier to harvest and as the fruit is well off the ground there is no chance that it will get mud splashed, nor will it be necessary to raise fruit on a layer of straw. You can improvise with a slightly lower 'table-top' system by setting a plank on two or three breeze blocks. Use a grow-bag as the growing medium, cutting holes in the plastic on its top and inserting short canes at an angle to the grow-bag to hold some of the fruiting stems apart, so that they all ripen well.

growing shrubby fruit

GOOSEBERRIES, RED- AND WHITECURRANTS AND THEIR HYBRIDS CAN ALSO BE FITTED INTO A
MIXED PLANTING SCHEME, BUT THEY WILL NEED REGULAR PRUNING TO KEEP FRUITING WELL.

Currants and gooseberries are available as stool bushes,
where the stems come straight from the root system or
as bushes with a leg and several stems growing from it.
These plants can be trained into fan shapes to grow
against walls, fences or the sides of garden buildings or
they can be pruned into roughly U-shaped bushes, where
their centres are open and allow good air circulation.

gooseberries

Gooseberries (*Ribes grossularia*) are also available, or can
be trained, as taller standards with round heads. These are
useful in an ornamental sense to provide height and raise
eye-level in a low-level herb or kitchen garden.

Choices: 'Careless' and 'Invicta' have well-deserved
reputations as heavy cropping and vigorous growing
plants, and 'Invicta' is immune to mildew. 'Whinham's
Industry' produces good-flavoured fruit and the extra
attraction is that the fruit ripens to a dark red.

redcurrants

Redcurrant (*Ribes vulgare*) fruits hang from the plant in
clusters, like glistening red and white jewels.

Choices: The best choice for redcurrants is 'Rovada', with
large clusters of fruit in late summer. 'Jonkheer van Tets'
and 'Stanza' also provide abundant fruit in late summer.
For variation grow whitecurrant 'White Versailles'.

ABOVE *Blueberry 'Bluecrop'.*

The fruits gleam like large yellowish raindrops on the bushes and are ready to pick in summer.

Prune gooseberries and currants to keep an open shape, with good air circulation at the centre of the plant. The plants should look like a vase in outline. Once you have the shape, prune off two-thirds of the length of remaining branches, to leave a pair of buds going to the left and right of the stem. Remove any suckers that appear at the base of the plants in summer, by pulling them off the plant.

blackcurrants

Blackcurrants (*Ribes nigrum*) can be used to make a simple hedge at the edge of a vegetable plot. At the time of planting cut stems back to buds at about 5–10 cm (2–4 in) above ground level. In later years, when plants are growing well, cut back fruiting stems when you harvest and others by a third.

Choices: Many disease- and frost-resistant cultivars exist, including 'Ben Sarek'.

blueberries

Blueberries (*Vaccinium* spp.) need acid soil conditions to fruit well. If your soil conditions are not suitable, provided you have the space for two varieties (necessary for good pollination), you can grow them in large pots in the garden or on a patio. If you do have acid soil conditions, blueberry bushes will look attractive in spring with their tiny white bell flowers, be productive in summer and in autumn their foliage will provide burnished colour.

Blueberry plants can grow up to 1.5–1.8 m (5–6 ft) and take a number of years before they fruit. Some are self-fertile, but planting two varieties ensures better pollination.

Prune blueberry bushes once they are well established, after four years. For the first pruning, take out weak and spindly stems and those that cross. Otherwise only take out up to a quarter of stems that have fruited each year.

Choices: 'Bluecrop' grows into an upright shape and will do well in dry or well-drained, but moist conditions. 'Coville' ripens late in the season, while 'Earliblue' is at its best in midsummer.

FROST PROTECTION

Wall- or fence-trained fruit trees, such as cherries, peaches and apples will benefit from frost protection, which should increase fruit production.

1 Fix a wooden batten to the wall above the tree and tack material such as horticultural fleece, hessian or plastic into place. Keep it away from the tree by laying a few canes against the underside of the batten, with the lower ends of the canes pushed into the ground.

2 Tie the vertical sides of the material onto the canes and weight the bottom end on the ground using stones or bricks. By day, move the fabric off the blossoms so they can be pollinated.

growing cane fruits

RASPBERRIES, BLACKBERRIES, JAPANESE WINEBERRIES AND HYBRIDS, SUCH AS
LOGANBERRY, SUNBERRY, TUMMELBERRY AND TAYBERRY, NEED STRONG AND PERMANENT
SUPPORTS FOR THEIR RAMBLING OR WHIPPY FRUITING STEMS.

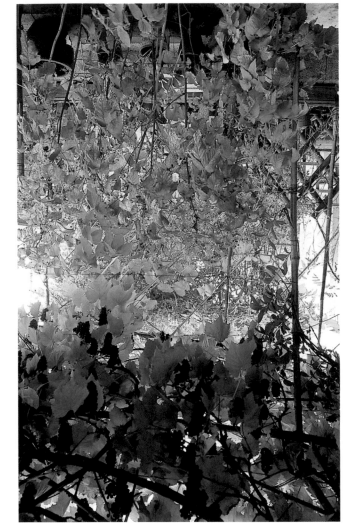

ABOVE Raspberry canes frame an archway on a grape-shaded patio.

raspberries

The raspberry (*Rubus idaeus*) offers luscious fruits in summer and in autumn. The autumn fruits come from new season's growth, so cut canes right to the ground each winter to produce new canes that won't fruit in summer, but will be ready in autumn.

A group of 4–6 raspberry canes, supported by tall bamboo canes, makes a centrepiece for a formal kitchen garden that is both decorative and productive. Tie the fruit canes into the bamboo canes at regular intervals, and make sure the supporting structure is secure, by tying the bamboo canes together with lightweight garden wire.

Choices: Best summer fruit choices are 'Glen Cova' and 'Glen Moy' with 'Golden Everest', a yellow-fruiting form. Raspberries that fruit in autumn, bringing all the fragrance of summer-fruiting cultivars, include 'Autumn Bliss', 'Fallgold' and 'Zeva'.

blackberries

Blackberries (*Rubus fruticosus*) grow best in full sun in well-drained but moist sites. Enrich the soil before planting with well-rotted manure. Set the plants in place at the base of the fencing or support system and cut the plants back to 20 cm (8 in). As the canes grow, train them into the supports and each year, in winter cut out the canes that fruited during the year. Mulch the soil around

RIGHT Loganberries, which are blackberry hybrids, produce sharp-tasting fruits.

hybrid berries

The hybrid berries are crosses between blackberries and raspberries and other Rubus species. They vary in colour, from purple through to pink and red. Blackberries and their hybrid berries (which include the loganberry, silvanberry, sunberry, tayberry and tummelberry) are all heavy cropping and good tasting. They can be used in similar decorative and productive ways to produce summer fruits. However, they all need space, in most cases about 2.4 m (8 ft), so unless you have a long fence to cover, it is likely that you will only be able to fit one or two plants into a kitchen garden.

In a mixed planting, though, you can use these plants for ornamental effect, or even practical purposes, to make a slim and productive hedge for part of the garden. Positioned well, the fruit 'hedge' may form a boundary between different parts of the garden. Blackberries and their hybrids and the Japanese wineberry can be trained over arched supports or wound around the pillars of a pergola.

the base of the plants with compost to reduce weeds and to retain moisture. In dry seasons water the bushes as the berries begin to turn purple.

Choices: 'Fantasia' is a new variety of blackberry growing on a vigorous plant which bears very heavily and has good flavour, tasting very much like the wild blackberry. 'Loch Ness' is a thornless, well-flavoured blackberry which crops well. 'Oregon Thornless' has all the attributes of cultivated blackberries but in addition provides attractive autumnal foliage colour. For attractive flowers grow 'Veronique', which has pink blooms and is thornless.

chapter six:

vegetable circle garden
semi-circular vegetable garden
potager-style garden
rooftop container garden
fruit garden

6

garden plans

THERE ARE SOME LAYOUTS THAT SUIT KITCHEN GARDENS PARTICULARLY WELL, AND THESE CAN BE EASILY ADAPTED TO FIT INDIVIDUAL SITUATIONS. THE IDEA IS TO GET THE MOST OUT OF EVERY BIT OF BARE EARTH, PATIO OR ROOFTOP.

vegetable circle garden

Circles are popular shapes for ornamental flower gardens and herb gardens, and in the small garden they suit a particular vegetable and for successional sowing. The overall outline is of a wheel, with divisions that resemble the spokes of a wheel. A circular bed is easy to see at a glance, and its shape allows you easy access for weeding and harvesting from the outer edges. However, when you need to work at the centre of the circle you should avoid walking directly on the soil, so allow space for either stepping stones or narrow paths for you to tread on.

vegetable growing well. A circle can be divided into diamond or wedge-shaped sections, and further sub-divided into smaller sections for planting small quantities

the layout

The circular plot shown here has a diameter of 3 m (10 ft) and is divided into an inner and outer circle, with a central planting area holding a collection of runner beans, and providing a decorative focal point for the circle. Using string and wooden pegs, divide the circle into six segments. Similarly, with a shorter piece of string mark out the circumference of the inner circle.

The outer circle has stepping stones placed at regular intervals in between the vegetable sections. By standing on them you can weed and maintain the inner circle of vegetables without compacting the soil.

the wigwam

Put in place the canes for the central bean wigwam. Push the ends firmly into the ground so that the structure is stable and tie the tops securely in place. Wind string around the wigwam at intervals up the length of the canes, to provide additional footholds for the climbing beans.

planting

You can choose to grow varying amounts of a particular vegetable within each segment or its subdivision. As one small block of vegetables is harvested you can replace it with seeds, seedlings, or young plants of a second crop.

LEFT *Grow as much as you can within the confines of the circular vegetable garden by using the central area to grow a climbing crop. You can either use traditional supports, a typical garden object such as a climbing frame or even an old ladder to hold the tough stems and heavy fruits of squash or pumpkin.*

planting a vegetable circle

for the centre

1 Beans: there are at least six canes, with three plants per cane (one on each side of the cane) – 'Relay' which has white, pink and red flowered varieties in the seed mix, 'Cosse Violette' (purple pods), 'Corona d'Oro' (yellow pods), 'Painted Lady' (pretty white and red flowers) and 'Blue Lake' (green pods). Surround the bean wigwam with a circle of parsley and chives or spring onions.

outer parts of the circle

2 Lettuces: grow several varieties, varying them as you harvest. Grow six blush-types with purple/green markings such as 'Little Leprechaun', six cos types such as 'Little Gem' and six oakleaf types such as 'Red Salad Bowl' or 'Salad Bowl' (green leaves). Follow lettuces with winter leeks.

3 Turnips: two rows of 'Atlanta', followed by spicy oriental greens, mizuna and mustard 'Red Giant', which will over-winter.

4 Carrots: grow two rows near the centre of the outer circle, with nine onion sets at the edge of the circle or six, if larger onions are wanted.

5 Chard: grow two rows selecting from Swiss chard (green foliage and stems), Ruby Chard (red) or Bright Lights (rainbow colours in stems and leaves).

6 Radish: sown in a random broadcast of seed, followed in summer by one or, at most, two courgette plants.

7 Beetroot: grow two rows of 'Chioggia Pink' or 'Boltardy'.

3 m (10 ft) diameter

semi-circular vegetable garden

Using a circular shape as its basis, the semi-circle enables you to take advantage of odd areas in the garden and you could even extend it into a three-quarter circle, butting onto a path or against the side of the house. This is also a perfect shape to use against the back wall of a town garden.

marking out

To mark it out, put in place two canes at either end of the straight, back edge of the semi-circle. Mark the middle, put a cane in place and then with a piece of string half the length of the straight side, mark out the circumference of the semi-circle.

edgings and paths

Edge the bed with a path for ease of access. It is also useful to have a stepping stone or chequer-board path at the rear if the semi-circle backs onto a wall or fence so you can work at the back of the bed without compacting the soil. In any case, the area immediately by the wall will be dry, making it difficult to grow vegetables close up to it. If you use a chequer-board, stepping stone approach to the path at the back, plant herbs such as chives, oregano and thyme into the spaces between the pavers or stepping stones. Put in place a few stepping stones within the bed itself, so that you can have easy access without damaging plants and soil by treading on them.

RIGHT *Arrange canes in a short row that follows the lines of a semi-circular plan to contrast with the curves at the front of the garden.*

planting

The semi-circle is roughly divided into segments, but some crops are planted in rows that cross several segment divisions. At the centre and to the back of the semi-circle, to give height and a focal point, grow runner beans supported on canes. Instead of arranging canes in a traditional wigwam shape, you could vary the central focus by growing the beans in a short row, placing the canes in a line. Leave enough space between the beans and the back wall to enable you to get behind the canes to harvest the crop.

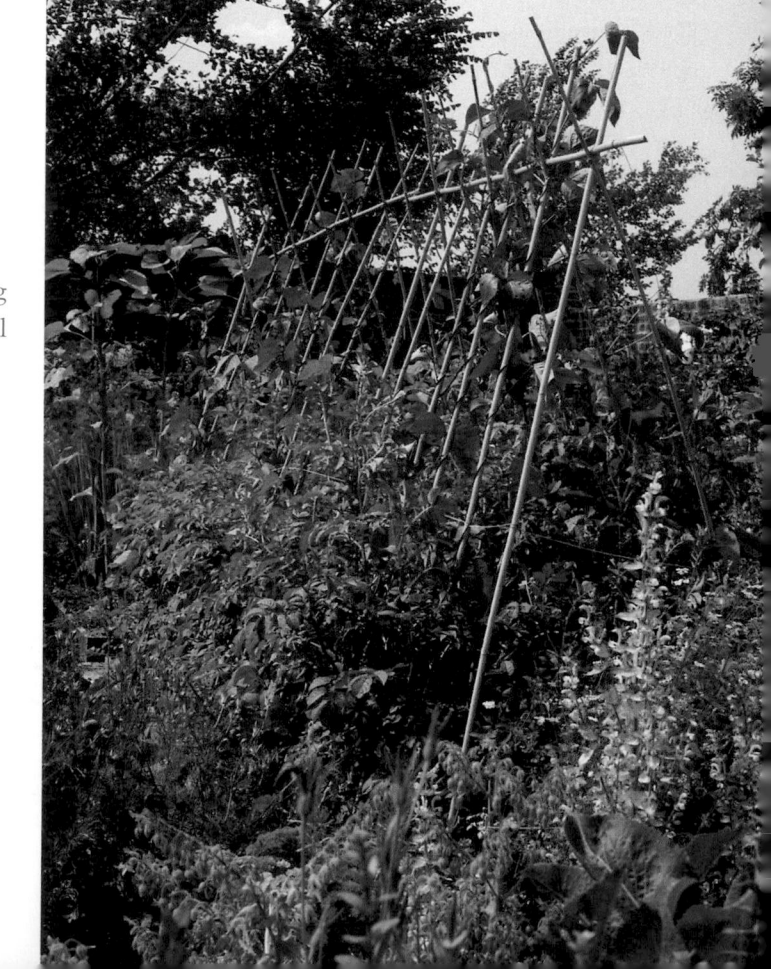

plant list

1. Chives.
2. Oregano.
3. Thyme.
4. Chervil.
5. Runner beans 'Painted Lady' and 'Relay' for a variety of flower colour.
6. Swiss chard ('Bright Lights' for multi-coloured effect or plain green 'Lucullus' or red 'Burgundy Chard').
7. Ornamental cabbage (colourful, edible varieties are available).
8. Onion sets 'New Fen Globe'.
9. Sprouting broccoli (green 'Early White Sprouting' and purple form 'Early Purple Sprouting').
10. Carrots 'Parmex' or 'Parabell'.
11. Beetroot 'Boltardy' or 'Monogram'.
12. Radish 'Cherry Belle' or 'Scarlet Globe' (once harvested, sow more lettuce or Oriental greens).
13. Lettuce (mixed plantings of different colours) 'Salad Bowl' (green), 'Little Leprechaun' (mauve/purple).
14. Two courgette plants (one green form 'Ambassador' and one yellow-skinned form 'Taxi', 'Gold Rush' or 'Jemmer').
15. Oriental greens (broadcast seed).
16. Two peppers 'Big Banana' (plant out only when all danger of frost is over).
17. Two tomatoes 'Golden Sunrise' and 'Sweet cherry'.

1.5 m (5 ft)

potager-style garden

Angular shapes, such as triangles and squares, are popular choices for containing formal vegetable gardens. Each bed is in essence a raised bed, edged with boards and filled with soil and compost. This design can be used as part of a rotation where you move crops from square to square annually.

If space permits you can fit all four squares into your garden; if not reduce the number of squares to two and divide each into four, so that you can still grow the same range of vegetables, even if in smaller quantities.

the layout

The four squares in this formal vegetable garden are divided by a path 45–60 cm (1½–2 ft) wide – broad enough to work from and to push a wheelbarrow along. When laying out the garden, measure out the beds and secure the treated wooden boards in place, then add the soil and compost to each bed and fork it over well, allowing it to settle before planting up.

making the paths

Remove stones and weeds from the area which is to become the paths and lay a woven plastic membrane. This dark material blocks out light and weakens any weed seedlings or perennial weeds that start to grow. On top of the membrane add a layer of gravel or bark to reduce the likelihood of weed seedlings coming through and to provide a finished, ornamental look to the design. The membrane is permeable so water will filter through, becoming available in the soil for the vegetable plants.

LEFT *Although the boards enclosing the raised beds will hold most plants away from the paths, you can ensure that large vegetable foliage is held off by placing low, decorative hoops or hurdles inside the boards.*

planting a potager-style garden

❶ Roots

Three rows of potatoes 'Mimi' or
   'Dunluce'.
One row of carrots 'Early Market'.
One row of parsnip 'Tender and True'.

❷ Brassicas and onions

Kale 'Redbor' (one row taking up
   45 cm/18 in).
Kohlrabi 'Purple Delicacy' and
   'Green Delicacy'.
Two rows of onions 'Centurion'.

❸ Peas and beans

Double row of sugar peas 'Sugar
   Rae', with twigs in place to
   support the crop as it grows.
Three rows of dwarf French beans in
   a range of pod colours: 'Royalty'
   (purple), 'Canadian Wonder'
   (green) and 'Sungold' (yellow).

❹ Salads and Chinese greens

Lettuce 'Red Salad Bowl' or 'Marvel
   of Four Seasons'.
Salad rocket.
Several rows of mixed lettuces and
   cut-and-come-again mixtures.
Two rows of Chinese greens
   (mizuna, mibuna, purple mustard,
   Pak choi).

1.5 m (5 ft)   45–65 cm   1.5 m (5 ft)
         (1½–2 ft)

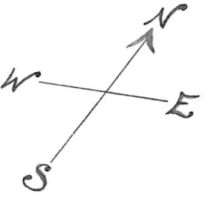

rooftop container garden

Even in the confined spaces of a rooftop, it is possible to grow a range of vegetables and herbs that will provide both tasty produce and ornamental qualities. You will not be able to grow in quantity, but by choosing the vegetables you like most you will be able to keep a succession going, bringing on new plants for those already harvested.

containers

The secret of success lies in having the largest containers you can safely site on the roof or balcony. You may need to reinforce the roof and for this you will need professional advice. Large containers offer more space in this already space-hungry site, but they don't need watering daily, which reduces maintenance. However, size does mean weight, so be sure you have the container sited correctly before you fill it with compost.

If safety constraints and access allow, put in place raised, waist-high planting systems which run around the outline of the roof. You could also group containers together, in same-plant selections or in a random arrangement of vegetables, in much the same way as you would plan a decorative collection.

grow-bags

Some containers, such as grow-bags, are functional and not overly attractive, but if they fulfil their use well, they are forgiven their looks. Watering can be a problem, as water usually spills out of the planting holes, bringing with it some of the compost. If using grow-bags for tomatoes, avoid this by planting them in bottomless pots and sinking these into the grow-bag. When you water, aim the hose into the pot rather than into the grow-bag.

space

Space is naturally at a premium so plantings go upwards as well as horizontal, and hanging baskets and window boxes are essential elements of the rooftop garden. They must be securely fixed if they overhang the street or a neighbour's patio or balcony.

shelter

On a rooftop or balcony wind may cause problems, so some form of shelter will be needed. You can fix trellis on a batten and secure this on the inside of the exterior wall of the roof, so that it is higher than the wall. Similarly, glass screens secured in place, although expensive, will reduce the vigour of the wind and increase the warmth of the site, without losing the views around it.

plants and containers

❶ Hanging baskets suit herbs, nasturtiums and trailing tomatoes.

❷ Chives with lettuce.

❸ Grow beans on canes in combination with lettuces at the front of a long, wide planter.

❹ A deep, round container holding cut-and-come-again lettuce and spring onions grown around Tomato 'Sun Belle'.

❺ Large tub for courgette 'Taxi' (yellow skin).

❻ In a large round container grow two pepper plants combined with violas, whose flowers can be used in salads.

❼ A deep and long container for carrots, sugar snap peas, and a few ornamental cabbages.

❽ Use a large square planter, with good drainage to hold a mixture of kohlrabi 'Purple Delicacy' and the oriental green, mizuna.

OPPOSITE *Grow fruit trees including apples, peaches and citrus in a sheltered position on the balcony or patio.*

fruit garden

If fruit is your preference, it is possible to fill a small garden and an adjoining patio with a sufficient variety of fruits to provide delicious produce as well as ornament in the form of flowers, fruit and, very often, autumn foliage.

the layout

The design shown here is for a 10 x 10 m (30 x 30 ft) plot and would fill the whole of a typical urban back garden, being both productive and highly attractive.

The suntrap of the patio allows you to grow fan-trained nectarine and cherry on opposite walls and a grapevine trained against the wall and over the back door. Figs and blueberry plants are grown in large wooden containers such as half-barrels and strawberries are grown in waist-high, table-top containers. The edge of the paved patio is lined with a low-growing, step-over planting of apples, separated by a central wrought iron archway, which supports a blackberry on one side and a boysenberry on the other, leading out into the garden.

Lining a path or simply planted into beds cut out of the grass is a row of fruit trees grown as half standards, including whitecurrants, redcurrants, pinkcurrants and gooseberries.

At the end of the line of half standards is an arbour with a fan-trained cherry on the back wall. Two lemon verbenas, grown as standards, are in pots at the edge of the arbour area, which can be underplanted with thyme, which will release its aroma as you walk over the foliage.

Growing along the two sides of the fruit garden are a collection of apples and pears to the left, and on the right a selection of raspberries. On the far boundary of the garden, against the wall or fence are tayberries, jostaberries and a blackcurrant, while a Victoria plum completes the tree fruit selection in the far corner on the right-hand side.

LEFT *If fruit is your delight, every available surface including walls and fences will become a site for training plants such as this fan-shaped morello cherry.*

plants for a fruit garden

The initials in brackets behind apples and pear varieties indicate the pollinating group they come from and therefore their compatibility.

❶ Patio

1 Fig.
2 Grape.
3 Strawberries: six plants of Fragaria variegata and six plants of 'Cambridge Late Pine'.
4 Blueberry 'Earliblue'.
4 Blueberry 'Coville'.
5 Fan-trained cherry 'Morello'.
6 Fan-trained nectarine 'Lord Napier'.
7 Step-over apple hedge 'Lord Derby' (c).
8 Step-over apple hedge 'Charles Ross' (b).

❷ Arch

9 Boysenberry.
10 Blackberry.

❸ Left-hand boundary

11 Apple 'Worcester Pearmain' (b).
12 Pear 'William' (c).

13 Pear 'Doyenne' (d).
14 Pear 'Beth' (d).
15 Pear 'Concorde' (c).
16 Apple 'Howgate Wonder' (c). These are grown as cordons on a post and fence system, spaced 75 cm (2 ft 6 in apart).

❹ Back wall

17 Plum 'Victoria'.
18 Tayberry 'Buckingham'.
19 Fan-trained cherry 'Stella'.
20 Lemon verbena grown as standards in containers.
21 Jostaberry.
22 Blackcurrant 'Ben Sarek'.

❺ Right-hand boundary

23 Raspberry 'Autumn Bliss': five plants.
24 Raspberry 'Fall Gold': five plants.

❻ Row of half standards in lawn

25 Whitecurrant 'White Versailles'.
26 Pinkcurrant 'Pink Jean'.
27 Redcurrant 'Stanza'.
28 Redcurrant 'Jonkheer van Tets'.
29 Gooseberry 'Invicta'.
30 Gooseberry 'Whinham's Industry'.

growing times

Spring is the traditional sowing time but there are many varieties that offer later or earlier harvests, extending the season, and there are a number of plants that you can sow several times in succession, so that you have a continuity of harvest. When you sow depends on where you live, and what the very local weather conditions of your own garden's micro-climate are like. If you have a greenhouse or a sunny windowsill you can start sowing earlier and harden the seedlings off in a cold frame before planting out when the conditions permit. The chart below shows guidelines to sowing and harvesting. Any plant with an asterisk next to it can be sown all year round.

Under glass/protected   Sow outdoors   Windowsill   ● When to sow   ● When to harvest   * All year round as a salad leaf

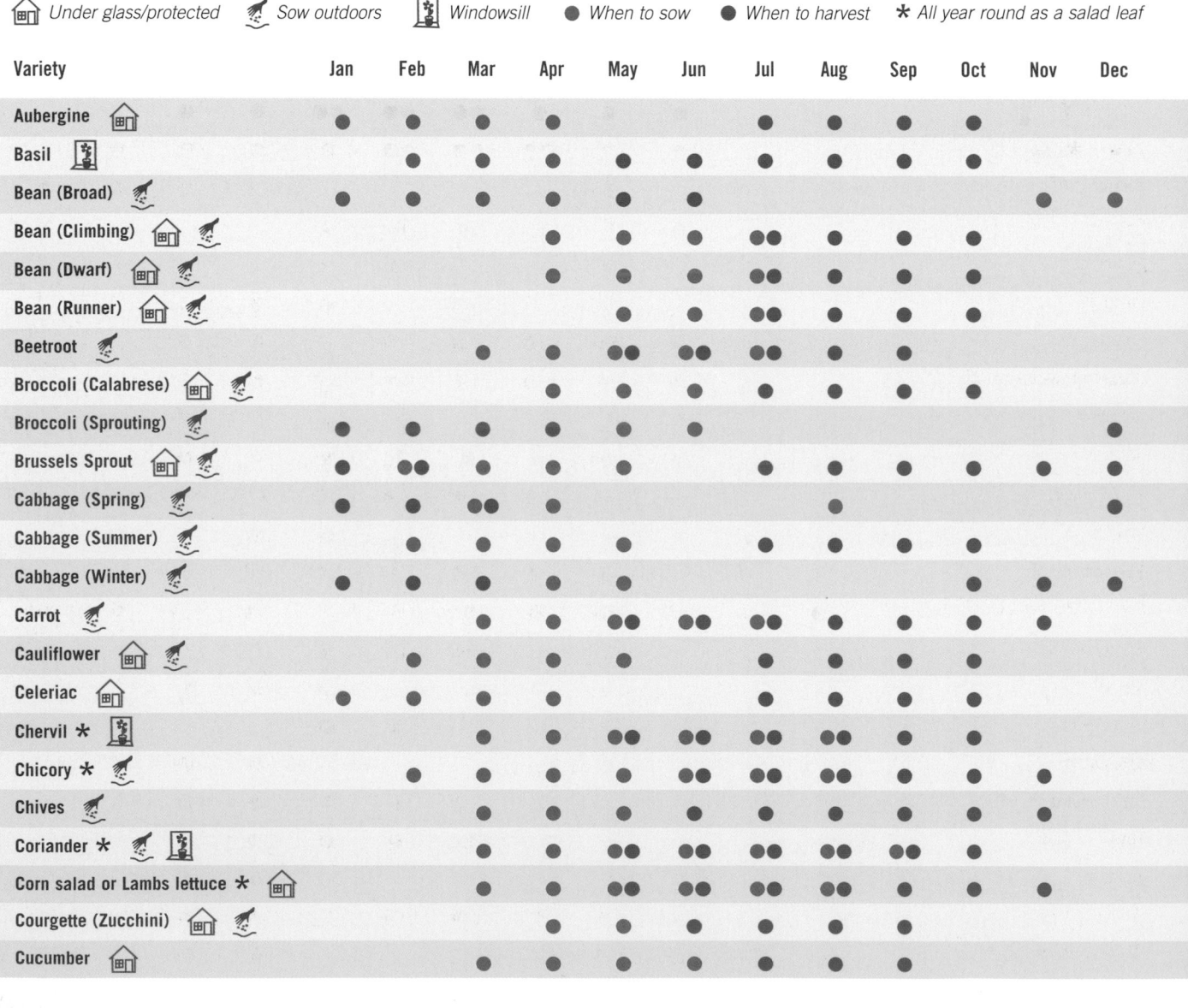

Variety	Jan	Feb	Mar	Apr	May	Jun	Jul	Aug	Sep	Oct	Nov	Dec
Aubergine	●	●	●	●			●	●	●	●		
Basil		●	●	●	●	●	●	●	●	●		
Bean (Broad)	●	●	●	●	●		●	●	●	●	●	●
Bean (Climbing)					●	●	●●	●	●	●		
Bean (Dwarf)					●	●	●●	●	●	●		
Bean (Runner)					●	●	●●	●	●	●		
Beetroot			●	●	●●	●●	●●	●	●	●		
Broccoli (Calabrese)				●	●	●	●	●	●	●		
Broccoli (Sprouting)	●	●	●	●								●
Brussels Sprout	●	●●	●	●	●			●	●	●	●	●
Cabbage (Spring)	●	●	●●	●				●				●
Cabbage (Summer)		●	●	●				●	●	●		
Cabbage (Winter)	●	●	●	●	●				●	●	●	●
Carrot				●	●●	●●	●●	●	●	●	●	
Cauliflower		●	●	●			●	●	●	●		
Celeriac	●	●	●	●			●	●	●	●		
Chervil *		●	●	●●	●●	●●	●●		●			
Chicory *		●	●	●	●	●●	●●	●●	●	●	●	
Chives		●	●	●	●	●	●	●	●	●		
Coriander *		●	●	●●	●●	●●	●●	●●	●			
Corn salad or Lambs lettuce *		●	●	●●	●●	●●	●●	●	●	●		
Courgette (Zucchini)			●	●	●	●	●	●	●			
Cucumber		●	●	●	●	●	●	●	●			

Variety	Jan	Feb	Mar	Apr	May	Jun	Jul	Aug	Sep	Oct	Nov	Dec
Dill *			●	●	●	●●	●●	●	●			
Kale *	●	●	●	●			●	●	●	●	●	●
Kohlrabi			●	●	●●	●●	●●	●	●	●		
Leek	●	●●	●	●					●	●	●	●
Lettuce (All year round)	●	●	●●	●●		●●	●●	●	●	●		
Mangetout pea			●	●	●	●	●	●				
Marjoram			●	●			●	●	●			
Melon				●	●		●	●	●			
Onion		●	●	●				●	●			
Pak choi *			●	●		●●	●●	●●	●	●		
Parsley *			●	●	●●	●●	●	●	●	●	●	
Parsnip	●	●●							●	●	●	●
Pea			●	●	●	●●	●	●				
Pepper		●	●	●			●	●	●	●		
Pumpkin				●	●		●	●	●			
Radish			●	●	●●	●●	●●	●●	●	●		
Rocket (Arugula) *			●	●	●●	●●	●●	●●	●	●		
Rosemary			●	●	●		●	●	●			
Sage			●	●			●	●	●	●		
Salad leaves *			●	●●	●●	●●	●●	●●	●●	●●	●	
Shallot		●	●	●					●	●		
Spinach *			●	●	●●	●●	●	●●	●●	●		
Spinach (Perpetual)	●	●●	●●	●●	●	●	●	●	●●	●●	●	●
Spring onion			●	●	●	●●	●●	●	●	●		
Squash				●	●		●	●	●			
Strawberry	●	●	●	●			●	●				
Sweetcorn				●	●				●	●		
Swiss chard *			●	●	●	●●	●	●	●	●		
Thyme			●	●			●	●	●	●		
Tomato			●	●				●	●			
Turnip			●	●	●	●●	●●	●	●	●		
Watercress *	●	●●	●●	●●	●				●	●	●	●

harvesting

SO THE SEEDS WERE PLANTED IN SPRING, THE SEEDLINGS THINNED OR TRANSPLANTED, AND

NOW YOU HAVE BEEN WAITING PATIENTLY FOR THEM TO REACH MATURITY, READY FOR HARVEST.

As the season progresses bean and pea pods start developing, marrows, courgettes and squash start to swell, and beetroot and other root vegetables begin to show at the soil surface. As you walk around the garden, notice each stage of development: make a practice of comparing day-to-day developments, something that is almost second nature when you have been growing your own fruit, vegetables and herbs for many years. You will be able to notice the subtle changes as skin colour deepens, shapes change and the harvest moment approaches.

Pick a pod from your French beans and see if it snaps, signalling the harvest start; make a mark on a sweetcorn or check whether you can see the peas in the pod. All these signs will point towards the most satisfying activity in the garden year, that of harvest, using and preserving.

Whichever part of the plant you harvest, it is part of the plant's own strategy for survival. Plants need leaves to manufacture chlorophyll, fruits to hold the seeds of next year's plants, and roots of plants such as carrots, parsnips and potato tubers are its own storage organs.

You have to allow the plant to get to a certain point in the development of its leaves, roots, flowers, fruits or seeds before you can step in and harvest. If you don't harvest, the plant will go on making its own survival plans. In the case of beans, for instance, if you leave the pods on the plant and the seeds begin to swell and set, then the plant will have achieved its aim of providing future seeds and will stop flowering. You have to pick the pods just before this stage, so that the plant keeps on producing flowers and then pods, which will ultimately benefit you.

vegetables for the small garden

There are so many wonderful vegetables to choose from. Grow the vegetables you enjoy the most and harvest them at their peak of perfection to eat fresh, or preserve for future meals.

Artichokes: globe artichokes are ready for harvest when the head is 10 cm (4 in) in diameter. What you are picking is the closely packed flower bud, well before it is ready to flower. Pick the largest one first,

from the leading shoot. This encourages the others to grow larger and you can harvest about 8 to 10 artichoke heads from mature plants in early summer and younger plants in late summer.

Beans (broad): pick early pods in June, and as they are small and tender, you can cook the whole pod. For the maincrop, pick pods when you can just see the outline of the beans swelling within the pods. If you open a pod, check that the beans look a good size. Some varieties, including 'Listra' and 'Optica' can be used as you would mangetout peas, by boiling and eating the pods and immature beans inside them.

Beans (French): their nickname, snap beans, should tell you that they are ready for harvest when the pods snap easily if you bend them. When this happens and the pods are about 10 cm (4 in) long, pick everyday. Use a pair of scissors or pinch the stalks off by hand, but never pull the pods off or you may uproot or damage the entire plant.

Beans (runner): don't let the bean pods get too long. Start picking when they are 15 cm (6 in) long and pick regularly. If you leave them on the plant and they get mature, the plant will stop flowering and therefore stop producing a succession of beans for you to harvest.

Beetroot: lift when you see their necks begin to swell near the soil surface. Don't let the beetroot get larger than 8 cm (3.5 in) or they will have lost their soft texture and will be woody and tasteless.

Carrots: there are many different carrots and several cultivars that mature early, but the maincrop can be left in the soil and harvested over winter, or lifted and stored from October onwards.

Broccoli (Calabrese): pick the main heads from the top of the plant when the florets are well formed and tightly packed on the stem, but before any of the small flowers actually open. If they do, they can still be used but the flavour and look is not so good. Picking encourages the good growth of the side heads.

Brussels sprouts: October is the time to begin the harvest, when the lower leaves start to turn yellow. Harvest the sprouts at the base of the stems first, then later move up the stem to the sprouts at the top. Leave a few stems unpicked and lift the whole stem before Christmas to use all the sprouts on it for a festive lunch.

Cabbage: with so many different types available you can be harvest cabbage all through the year, but from June to September, summer and autumn cabbages are at their best for eating fresh. Pick when the heads are large enough for your needs and are firm to the touch.

Cauliflower: once again, there are so many cultivars that this is no longer simply an autumn crop. Don't let the heads get too big before you starting using them. They should be compact and densely packed.

Cucumbers: by August you should have sampled much of your outdo or crop. Pick regularly once the fruits have reached a good size,

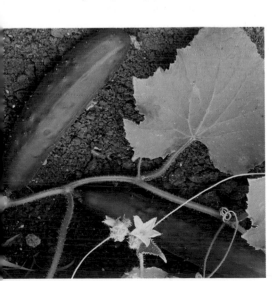

up to 30 cm (12 in) long. Regular picking encourages flower and cucumber production.

Lettuces and other salad leaves: with successional and protected sowing you can enjoy crunchy and colourful leaves over a long season. Cut whole lettuces when they have hearted up well and take leaves from cut-and-come-again varieties on a regular basis.

Marrows, courgettes, pumpkin and squash: marrows are really courgettes that got away and grew too large. Pick courgettes regularly once the fruits are 15 cm (6 in) long to keep the plant producing and try not to let the courgettes grow too large. Pick marrows when they are 30 cm (12 in) long. They can be kept through the summer. Summer squash, such as 'Patty Pan' and 'Scallopini' are picked when just

15 cm (6 in) in diameter or even smaller. Colourful and shapely fruits such as pumpkin and winter squash are used over winter and should be allowed to ripen on the vine. But if frost is forecast they need to be protected or picked and stored. Ideally though, after picking, their skins need to be ripened or cured for ten days in a sunny, frost-free site.

Onions, shallots and garlic: pick shallots when their leaves have died back and turned yellow from late July. Onion foliage turns down and begins to die back when the bulbs are reaching maturity. Leave them *in situ* for a fortnight, then lift them and either leave on the soil or in a dry site to dry off for up to three weeks if you are storing them; if not, you can begin to use them immediately. Always use first those that have thick necks or are slightly damaged. Lift garlic when the foliage begins to turn yellow, dry off and keep in a dry place until ready to use.

Parsnips: when their foliage begins to die down in autumn, begin harvesting. You can leave parsnips in the soil over the winter, but mark their position and cover with straw to make harvest easier after frost.

Peas: peas are ready to harvest when the peas as visible in the pod (maincrop), although mangetout peas should be picked when the peas are immature. Pick regularly, as pods

left to get mature on the plant will inhibit further cropping.

Potatoes: cut back the foliage and stems or haulm in September. By now, the foliage will be yellow and brown. You can leave the maincrop in the soil for a while but only if the crop is healthy and slugs are not a plague. Otherwise lift on a warm dry day and leave them to dry on the soil surface for up to 3 hours before storing them for later use.

Sweetcorn: pick cobs when the silky tassel at the top begins to turn a brown colour. For sweeter and more tender cobs, pick when they are not too large. Test an individual corn by making a dent in it with your thumbnail. If a milky white substance comes out, this is a sign that the cob is ready to harvest.

Tomatoes: as soon as the fruits start to ripen, it will be difficult to stop yourself picking these luscious summer treats! Let them ripen as much as possible on the plant, but if by September they are slow to ripen, there are several methods you can use to hurry them along: lay the plants, with their roots in the ground, on straw and protect the fruits with cloches, or pick the fruits and place them on trays in a warm greenhouse to ripen. Lastly, pack them into brown paper bags and keep them in dark, dry drawers to ripen.

fruit for the small garden

Apples, pears, plums and apricots can all be grown successfully in containers or in the ground, and soft fruits also do well in small spaces.

Apples and most top fruit are ready to pick for eating when they come away from the stalk just as you put your hand to hold them.

Soft fruit: you will have been harvesting in season the various summer fruiting varieties of raspberry and other soft fruits. And you will have autumn fruiting raspberries to look forward to. All are ready when they are well coloured and when they pull away from the stem easily.

herbs

The herb harvest for fresh leaves and flowers for salads and cooked dishes goes on all through the year, depending on the range of herbs you grow. But late summer is the time to harvest seeds of coriander, fennel and poppy if you plan to use them in baking, pickling or spicy cooking. Tarragon, parsley, sage, rosemary and thyme can all be harvested throughout the year but are at their best in summer (especially before flowering in the case of sage, rosemary and thyme) to use fresh or preserved for later use (by freezing, microwaving or drying).

preserving your produce

A PRODUCTIVE VEGETABLE GARDEN IS THE NATURAL SOURCE OF DELICIOUS, HOME-GROWN

PRODUCE. THERE'S NOTHING QUITE LIKE THE TASTE OF FRUIT OR VEGETABLES THAT YOU

HAVE JUST HARVESTED, PREPARED AND CAN EAT, RAW OR COOKED, THE SAME DAY.

Most vegetable growers will enjoy using this supply of fresh food, but there can be a surplus, known as a 'glut'. Most vegetables will keep well in the vegetable tray of the refrigerator for a period of time.

Before freezers were part of every home's kitchen furniture, vegetables were preserved in salt (runner beans), pickled in vinegar (onions and beetroot), dried (peas and beans) or kept in 'clamps' packed in dry, clean sand (root vegetables). With the arrival of the freezer, fruit and vegetables can be picked when they are at their best and frozen and stored for future use. Freeze as soon as possible after harvest. Work quickly, prepare all the vegetables as recipes or cookbooks instruct and have all the equipment clean, sterilized and ready for use in advance.

freezing

The key to successfully freezing fruit and vegetables is that once they are properly bagged up or boxed you need to label them clearly with the name of the produce and the date of freezing, so that you can identify them quickly and easily.

Vegetables such as broad beans, broccoli and celeriac can be open-frozen after blanching and cooling; this prevents them forming unmanageable clumps. Lay blanched vegetables onto baking sheets in the freezer, then, when frozen, transfer into freezer bags or plastic boxes, excluding as much air as possible.

You can also freeze cooked vegetables or made-up dishes, such as ratatouille. Tomatoes and onions flavoured with basil and made into sauces will be useful for pasta and pizza toppings. Convert surplus squash and pumpkin, leeks and potatoes into soups and freeze when cooled. Surplus apples can be made into a purée and frozen for use in desserts.

Some fruit, especially soft fruit, can be open-frozen without blanching. These include strawberries, cherries (remove stones), gooseberries, blackcurrants, red- and white currants, blackberries, mulberries and rhubarb.

BELOW Once you have open-frozen the soft fruit, mix together blackberries, raspberries and strawberries so that you have the makings of a summer pudding for later in the year.

blanching

Most vegetables, including sweetcorn, carrots, beans, courgettes and parsnips, need to be blanched before freezing. To do this, immerse the vegetables in boiling water for a couple of minutes, or longer depending on size. Remove them from the boiling water, tip them into ice-cold water, then drain, dry and freeze in bags, but only after they are completely cool.

making jams, jellies and chutneys

You can preserve many fruits and vegetables by making store cupboard preserves for use as sweet and savoury accompaniments. Fruits including apples, raspberries, blackberries, currants, plums and gooseberries are suitable for making jams and jellies. Strawberries, mulberries and morello cherries are among the fruits that have a low pectin content, so when using them you will need to use special sugar, known as 'jam' sugar, which has added pectin (or you can use liquid pectin instead).

Green tomatoes, courgettes, plums, apples, onions and chilli peppers (if you are brave), are all perfect ingredients for chutneys. Chutney is usually made with the addition of vinegar, so cook in stainless steel or aluminium pots as they don't react with vinegar.

When using fresh fruit and vegetables to make preserves, always cut away any damaged or blemished areas, and use the produce as fresh as possible. When the jams, jellies and chutneys are ready, ladle them into clean, sterilized jars with sterilized screw caps.

pickling

Cucumbers, beetroot and onions, as well as cauliflower, cabbage (sauerkraut) and beans (in piccalilli) are all suitable candidates for pickling. Preparation is the key, as ever, with

juicing

I use apples to make a delicious apple juice. First I clean, quarter, deseed and freeze the apples (the freezing process makes them easier to crush once they have been thawed out). Then I thaw out the apple pieces, place them in the apple press and squeeze all the juice out of them into containers. Finally, I put the juice through a sieve to remove any impurities, then I pour the juice into sterilized plastic bottles and freeze until needed.

Whichever method you use to preserve your garden harvests, remember to eat as much of the produce when it is fresh and at its best, soon after harvest, and then use up what is in your store cupboard as soon as possible, as there will soon be a follow-on harvest to take its place.

ABOVE Ladle jams, jellies, pickles and chutneys into clean, sterilized jars. Cover the surface with a waxed paper disc and leave to cool before closing the jar. Label with the name of the product and the date.

vegetables needing cleaning, skinning (if appropriate) and slicing or dicing. Always use vegetables in good condition.

protecting vegetable plants

IF YOU ENJOY GROWING VEGETABLES, YOU'LL WANT TO EXTEND THE GROWING SEASON SO THAT YOU HAVE BOTH EARLIER AND LATER CROPS. THIS CAN BE DONE BY PROTECTING PLANTS AGAINST TEMPERATURES LOWER THAN 6°C (43°F). HERE ARE SOME ESSENTIAL POINTERS TO MAKE SURE YOUR PLANTS ARE PROPERLY PROTECTED FROM COLD AND FROST.

protection from frost

The best protection from frost is available in the form of heated greenhouses and polytunnels. The cost factor of purchase and installation in both cases and the cost of heating the greenhouse will be the likely reasons against their use. But if you already have a greenhouse, then its use will justify the expenditure of heating as you will protect your crops in early spring and late in the season.

Unheated forms of protection, such as cloches and low plastic tunnels, will offer limited success in protecting plants from severe frost but they will be useful in less severe weather. Most forms of unheated protection will at least keep wind off plants and will keep them dry. They are easily stored, portable and simple to assemble, but the size of the plants will determine whether you choose low runs of cloche-style tunnels, a small polytunnel or tent-style cloche.

Fleece

Horticultural fleece is the best temporary protection and is relatively inexpensive. Usually sold in packs or by the metre from rolls, it is very light and can easily be floated over several rows of seedlings. You can also use it to cover existing mesh hoops. It won't be useful in severe winter conditions, but is a good first line of defence.

In spring, black fleece can be used to cover bare soil and raise the temperature so that seeds can germinate earlier. Once soil is warmed and you are sowing or planting into the ground, remove the black fleece. If you need to protect young plants and seedlings from weather and cold, use white fleece. Fleece covers need to be secured in place, either weighted down with stones or with pegs. Fleece is porous, so plants are not deprived of water as they grow. If you are generous with the fleece covering, there will be an allowance for the plants to grow upwards and raise it off the ground. Remove the fleece when frost danger is over and before the plants get too tall. You can re-use fleece, provided it is stored in a dry place until needed, and that it has not become too dirty or damaged during the first use.

Thawing out

Plants also need protection following frost when they are thawing out. Before the sun starts to thaw out the plants, cover them with an additional layer of fleece, which will slow down the thawing process.

shelter from wind and rain

Strong, drying or chilling winds affect vegetable plants. Wind damages plant growth because of its drying action on the foliage. It causes an increase of evaporation of water from the leaf which, if it happens too fast and too much water is lost, prevents the roots from replacing the water in the plant's vascular system, and so it is weakened and, in extreme cases, dies. Such damage, if the plant

ABOVE *Bamboo cloches are easy to move on and off plants that need protection from birds. You may need to peg them down in high winds.*

survives, will stunt its growth, causing it to grow in a misshapen way. What is more, windy conditions discourage the pollinating insects that are essential if fruit trees are to crop and certain flowers and vegetables are to set seed.

In a spacious site, hedges and shelter belts provide the best possible protection from wind and driving rain, but unless there is sufficient space, they will compete with the vegetables and fruit for nutrition and water from the soil.

Non-permeable covers

There are numerous styles and makes of non-permeable covers. Glass bell jars, plastic bell cloches and square Victorian glass cloches look elegant and are ideal for individual plants or small groups of seedlings, but you need to lift them for watering. Cloches such as these can be lifted and moved to parts of the garden where they are needed.

Customized cloches made from clear plastic 2-litre water bottles and large clear plastic containers are good cheap temporary protectors for individual seedlings. Cut off the base of the bottle or container and remove the top so that water and air can circulate.

protecting against bird damage

Bamboo and wire cloches won't be any use on their own as protection against cold weather, but they will protect individual plants or short rows of seedlings from foraging birds and they will allow free passage of water. In a frost you could place a layer of straw or conifer clippings around and over the plants to offer temporary protection.

Fruit crops, such as raspberries, strawberries, currants and other soft fruits, need protection from birds and if necessary, you may wish to protect them all together in a fruit cage, covered with heavy-duty netting.

Shiny aluminium strips, old CDs strung on wire or string between canes and mini-scarecrows all have their place in the fruit and vegetable grower's armoury, but they may be less than elegant and not fit into your overall design scheme.

pest protection

Barriers of fine mesh are useful for keeping insects and birds off the seedling and young plant stage of crops in spring. You can purchase this fine mesh made from UV-stabilized plastics in rolls from garden centres and specialist suppliers. It can be laid over crops on the ground, and over frames and hoops. The barriers will also offer a degree of protection against mild frosts and severe wind and rain. Although the fine mesh keeps insects out, it allows for air circulation and water flow, so plants continue to grow well. The netting should last for several seasons.

Carrot fly, which is a low-flying insect that homes in on the scent of carrots, celery, parsnips and parsley, can be controlled with a barrier around the sides of the crop rather than over the top. The fine-mesh screen masks the scents and becomes a barrier to the carrot fly.

further reading

Chef's Garden: Fresh Produce from Small Spaces, Terence Conran
(Conran Octopus, 1999)

Cool Green Leaves & Red Hot Peppers, Christine McFadden and
Michael Michaud (Frances Lincoln, 1998)

Creative Vegetable Gardening, Joy Larkcom (Mitchell Beazley, 1997)

Heritage Vegetables, The Gardener's Guide to Cultivating Diversity,
Sue Stickland (Gaia Books Ltd, 1998)

Matthew Riggs's Complete Book of Vegetables (Kyle Cathie Ltd, 1997)

Organic Gardening, Roy Lacey (David & Charles, 1988)

Pests: How to Control them on Fruit and Vegetables,
Pauline Pears and Bob Sherman (Henry Doubleday Research
Association/Search Press, 1992)

RHS Pests & Diseases: The Complete Guide to Preventing, Identifying
and Treating Plant Problems, Pippa Greenwood and Andrew Halstead
(Dorling Kindersley, 1997)

Roof Gardens, Balconies & Terraces, Jerry Harpur and David Stevens
(Mitchell Beazley 1997)

The Container Garden Month-by-Month, Jackie Bennett
(David & Charles, 1994)

The Container Kitchen Garden, Antony Atha (Collins & Brown, 2000)

The Edible Container Garden, Michael Guerra (Gaia Books Ltd, 2000)

The Gardener's Guide to Organic Gardening, Editor: Valerie Duncan
(Merehurst Ltd, 2000)

The Herb Garden Month-by-Month, Barbara Segall
(David & Charles, 1994)

The Kitchen Garden Month-by-Month, Andi Clevely
(David & Charles, 1996)

The New Kitchen Garden, Anna Pavord (Dorling Kindersley, 1996)

Urban Eden, Adam and James Caplin (Kyle Cathie Limited, 2000)

Vegetables, Ann Bonar (Tiger Books International, 1994)

Weeds: How to Control and Love Them, Jo Readman
(Henry Doubleday Research Association/Search Press, 1991)

Kitchen Garden magazine (www.magazine-group.co.uk)

picture credits

Mark Bolton: 38, 47. Jonathan Buckley: 7, 21, 66t, 73t. EWA:
90. Garden Picture Library/Photolibrary.com: 4/JS Sira, 9/John
Glover, 14t/R Sutherland, 14b/J Pavia, 16t F Strauss, 16b M
Lamontagne, 17/F Strauss, 20/Mayer/Le Scanff, 23/G Hanley,
26/E Peios, 32/JS Sira, 34 R Sutherland, 37 J Wade, 39 J Hurst, 40
J Wade, 45 L Brotchie, 46t L Brotchie, 46b M Watson, 48 F Strauss,
50 F Strauss, 51 N Holmes, 80 M Heuff, 82 F Strauss, 83 S Harte.
John Glover: 24, 33. Jerry Harpur: 41b, 81. Sunniva Harte: 86.
iStockphoto: 27, 28, 55, 56, 57t, 59, 60b, 61, 62, 63, 64, 65, 67, 68,
69, 70, 71, 72, 102, 103, 105, 106, 108, jacket. Andrew Lawson:
12, 36, 49, 73b, 76. Marianne Majerus: 6/+Barbara Schwarz, 15,
22, 79. Clive Nichols: 13, 18, 19, 41t/+Simon Irvine, 44,
54/+Hedens Lustgard, 58, 66b, 77. Photoshot: 84, 96, 98. Harry
Smith Collection: 60t, 78, 87, 92, 94. Sea Spring Photos: 57b.

useful addresses

garden centres and seed suppliers

UNITED KINGDOM

Association Kokopelli Organic Seeds
   www.terredesemences.com
Chiltern Seeds www.chilternseeds.co.uk
DT Brown www.dtbrownseeds.co.uk
Dobies www.dobies.co.uk
Highfield Nurseries www.highfield-nurseries.co.uk
Ken Muir www.kenmuir.co.uk
Kings Seeds www.kingsseeds.com
Marshalls Seeds www.marshalls-seeds.co.uk
Mr Fothergill's www.mr-fothergills.co.uk

Simpson's Seeds and Plants
   www.simpsonsseeds.co.uk
Suttons www.suttons.co.uk
The Organics Gardening Catalogue
   www.organiccatalog.com
Thompson & Morgan www.thompson-morgan.com
Unwins www.unwins.co.uk

UNITED STATES OF AMERICA

Bountiful Gardens www.bountifulgardens.org
Burpee www.burpee.com
Filaree Farm www.filareefarm.com
Johnny's Selected Seeds www.johnnyseeds.com
Seed Savers Exchange www.seedsavers.org

AUSTRALIA

GardenWay Home & Garden www.gardenway.com.au
Greengold www.greengold.com.au
Newman's Nursery www.newmansnursery.com.au
Digger's www.diggers.com.au

NEW ZEALAND

Kings Plant Barn www.kings.co.nz
McCully's Garden Centres
www.garden.christchurch.homeone.com.au

SOUTH AFRICA

Lifestyle Home Garden www.lifestyle.co.za

organizations

UNITED KINGDOM

Garden Organic www.gardenorganic.co.uk
The Royal Horticultural Society www.rhs.org.uk

AUSTRALIA

Brisbane Organic Growers Inc www.bogi.org.au
Canberra Organic Growers Society www.cogs.asn.au

websites

www.cityfarmer.org
www.edible.co.nz
www.expertgardener.com
www.garden.org
www.gardens.co.nz
www.garden-nz.co.nz
www.growinglifestyle.com
www.naturalhub.com
www.plantfinder.co.nz
www.windowbox.com

index